UNDERSTANDING YOUR HORSE'S LAMENESS

UNDERSTANDING YOUR HORSE'S LAMENESS

Diane E. Turner

ARCO PUBLISHING, INC.
219 PARK AVENUE SOUTH, NEW YORK, N.Y. 10003

ILLUSTRATED BY NANCY MANDOWA

Published by Arco Publishing, Inc.
219 Park Avenue South, New York, N.Y. 10003

Copyright © 1980 by Diane E. Turner

All rights reserved. No portion of this book may be reproduced by any means or in any form, without permission in writing from the publisher, except by a reviewer.

> **Library of Congress Cataloging in Publication Data**
>
> Turner, Diane E
>   Understanding your horse's lameness.
>
>   Bibliography: p. 142
>   Includes index.
>   1. Lameness in horses. I. Title.
> SF959.L25T87   636.1'08'9758   79-12687
>
> ISBN 0-668-04769-0 (Cloth Edition)

Printed in the United States of America

Andrea Phillips

Foreword

As we imagine the horse we must consider the innumerable centuries that have passed, filled with the usefulness of a creature so admired for its grace, its power and speed, that man devised to capture and contain the species only to find himself dependent on the beast for his own survival and improvement. It seems odd, however, that man, being so dependent on the many attributes of the horse, has learned so little about keeping that species functional.

A slowly growing knowledge of equine unsoundnesses and theories of their causes was accumulating until about fifty years ago when industrialization changed man's use for the horse from one of necessity to that of pleasure. We see the products of that recent change, from the "horse doctor" to the garage mechanic, from the iron horse shoe to the steel belted radial. In two to three generations we have gone from a vague but living comprehension of the causes and effects of equine lameness to a total bafflement concerning our horse's sore leg. The limited understanding of lameness held by our great-grandfathers is just not part of our dialogue and the gap leaves us totally uninformed and dependent on the specialized information of the veterinarian.

Today, one of the most discussed and least understood realities of equestrian life is unsoundness. This long overdue and most needed elaboration on the basics of horse lameness has been written by Diane Turner, a horse owner with the realization that a far too important topic has received far too little attention. The arrangement of this text will allow the reader an organized and informative review of the many aspects of equine lameness.

ROBERT E. CODY, JR., D.V.M.

Contents

    Foreword by Robert E. Cody, Jr., D.V.M.   5

    Preface   9

1. You, Your Vet, and Your Farrier   13
2. Your Horse   26
3. Joints, Tendons, Muscles, and Ligaments   35
4. Anatomy and Physiology of the Foot   43
5. Hoof Care   47
6. Equine Locomotion   49
7. Conformation   59
8. Lameness   81

    Diagnostic Charts   139

    Bibliography   142

    Index   143

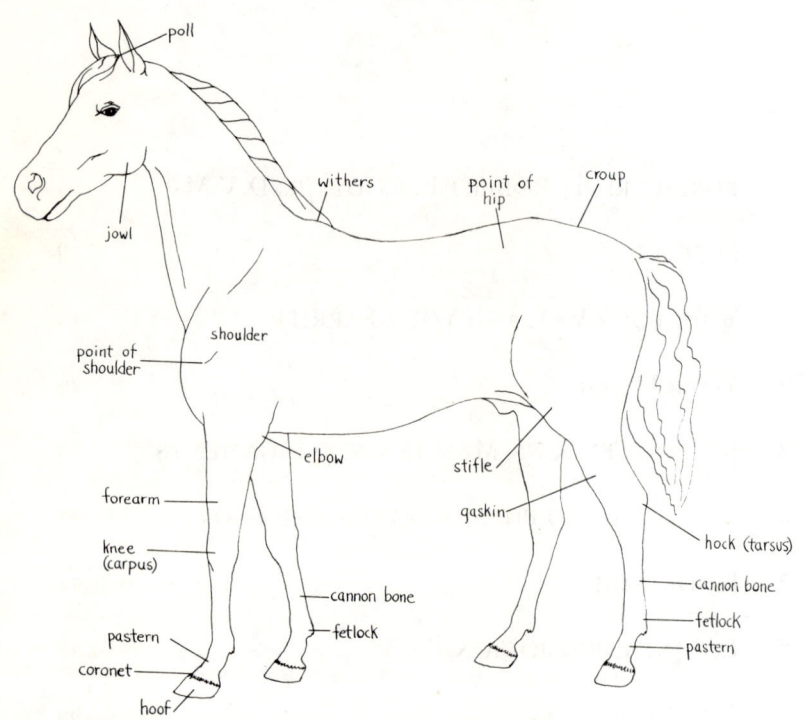

Preface

This book is designed to give the serious, concerned horse owner a clinical and diagnostic guide to the discovery, location, causes, and treatment of various kinds of lameness in horses. It is not intended to replace your veterinarian; if anything, the reader who studies it carefully should be all the more ready to call his vet at the first indication of trouble. What this book does try to do is to help the horse owner discover when serious trouble does occur, aid him in evaluating symptoms, and suggest some common courses of treatment.

Understanding Your Horse's Lameness is organized so as to let the owner begin at the beginning; it covers basic anatomy and conformation of the hoof and leg, movement mechanics of the horse, gaits, and proper examination techniques. Section II concerns various types of lameness: their definitions and causes, symptoms, and treatment. Most important, this book aims at the prevention of lameness, for many kinds of lameness can in fact be prevented. The key lies in good care, careful observation, and common sense—along with a good basic understanding of what makes a horse's legs work.

ACKNOWLEDGMENT

I would like to thank everyone who helped turn my dream into a book, most especially Dr. Robert E. Cody, D.V.M. He has been technical adviser, editor, critic, friend and the best horse veterinarian in the business.

I am also deeply indebted to my farrier, Lincoln Turner, who introduced me to many interesting horses and their feet.

Thanks also to Joan and Wally Buddington, Anne and Al Deckert, and Winnie and Charles Baldoff, all of whom took time from their busy schedules to help me with this book.

And of course, thanks to John, who filed and stacked and typed (and typed) and put up with me. This is his book too.

To Ed

ANATOMICAL TERMS

This book uses some fairly technical terminology referring to the location of structures in the horse's body and their position relative to each other. You should become acquainted with these terms to help your understanding of equine anatomy and lameness.

Posterior	Towards the tail, behind.
Anterior	Towards the head, in front.
Medial	Inside, towards the center.
Lateral	Towards the outside.
Proximal	Towards the vertebral column, above.
Distal	Away from the vertebral column, below.
Palmar	Towards the front of the foot.
Volar	Towards the top of the foot.
Superficial	Towards the surface.
Deep	Away from the surface.

CHAPTER 1

You, Your Vet, and Your Farrier

YOU

Not everyone should own a horse. For example, it is not everyone's cup of tea to clean out a stall at 6:00 A.M. in the freezing cold before going off to school or work. Nor is it especially exhilarating to walk a colicky horse for four hours in the middle of the night. And there are those who feel somewhat resentful at having to pay another vet bill when Trigger pulls up lame, particularly since the vet was out three days ago for the old boy's annual check-up and he was all right *then*.

This is not to say that owning a horse isn't any fun. It is. It is also a tremendous responsibility. A partial list of some of these responsibilities includes:

1. Providing your horse with a clean, dry stable, which is reasonably draft-free.
2. Feeding him regularly (two or three times a day). Water should be freely available to the horse at all times.
3. Brushing him often enough at least to keep the dirt and manure from caking and irritating the skin.
4. Looking at his teeth once in a while.
5. Picking his hoofs every day without fail.

6. Having him checked regularly by both a veterinarian and a farrier.

7. Exercising and resting him sufficiently, even if it means sometimes resting him when you want to ride and riding or longeing him when *you* feel like resting.

8. Having plenty of patience. Of all the qualities a conscientious horseowner needs, this is the most essential. To be patient means, in brief, not to be in such a big hurry. Not to give in to the temptation to ride your two-year-old, even if he is sixteen hands high. To forego the 38 supplements you want to feed your foal to make him grow faster. To take the time to check Dobbin's feet before you mount, and to look over that grassy field for holes before you go galloping over it. Groundhogs have a way of being very busy at night.

Since this is not a book on horse care or training (there are plenty of good ones available), no detailed consideration will be given to stabling, feeding, grooming, or exercising. If you are uncertain about basic equine care, learn all you can as soon as you can. Ignorance and neglect are two prime factors in horse lameness. And in most cases it's just as easy to do things the right way as the wrong way, and in the long run it's a good deal cheaper.

YOUR VET

The most important thing when it comes to vets is to have one, preferably before you buy your horse. Since prevention is the best medicine, the smartest thing to do is not to buy trouble. Many horse lamenesses are intermittent, especially in the early stages. Molly may have looked fine when you bought her, but if she comes down lame with navicular trouble in two months, don't be too surprised.

While your vet cannot necessarily prevent this, he can without doubt reduce the likelihood of its occurring. For a reasonable fee, most vets will be happy to go with you to examine your prospective purchase. Selecting a vet is somewhat simpler then selecting a horse, but do try to find one who specializes in large animals. Your search will be simplified, since many vets won't treat horses in any event. Remember, however, that in an emergency you should get any vet who is available, because any vet, even if he specializes in parakeets, can treat shock, for instance, better than you can.

After you have chosen your vet, the main thing is to be honest with him. This is not always as easy as it sounds. For example, if the vet asks you if you've been riding your horse hard on paved road, and you have (even though you know quite well that you shouldn't), *say* so. Doing the wrong thing and lying about it afterwards only complicates an already difficult problem in diagnosis. You may get a lecture (and so you should), but it won't kill you and you'll be helping the vet with his diagnosis, and so be helping your horse.

It is of paramount importance to learn to follow your vet's advice. If he recommends complete rest (for a stifle problem, say) then that is what is meant—not a jog around the pasture for a few minutes a day, but *complete rest*. If he wants you to give your horse light exercise, find out exactly what he means (trotting on a longe line, walk-trotting, or whatever) and then follow his directions. If he prescribes no exercise for two months, then resting the horse for six weeks is simply not long enough.

YOUR FARRIER

Whether or not you want shoes on your horse, you need a farrier. Although the term "blacksmith" is often used interchangeably with "farrier," there is a difference. A blacksmith is one who is skilled in ironwork; he may or may not know anything about shoeing horses. A farrier, on the other hand, is synonymous with "horseshoer," so that when you use this term, you know you are being correct. The farrier is just as vital to the welfare of your horse as the veterinarian.

Why are farriers needed? In the wild state, where horses spent a great deal of time on the move searching for new pastureland (and on the lookout for wolves) their hoofs were worn down naturally on the rocky trails. They did not require shoes, since they were not subjected to the unnatural weight of a rider; nor, of course, were they exposed to hard trotting on paved roads.

Today this situation is reversed. Many "back yard pets" are left to graze day after day in one pasture. They get little or no exercise and their hoofs grow far too long, developing cracks and separations. Or else they are ridden for long periods on hard roads which would ruin the hoofs of a barefoot horse in short order.

Whether ridden or not, your horse needs your farrier's attention every four to six weeks, starting when the foal is about two months old.

Choosing a farrier can be a difficult task. There are a great many horseshoers who are underqualified for this exacting art, so the burden falls upon the horse owner to find a good one. It is important to realize that, while a qualified farrier can correct or alleviate many horse lamenesses, a hack can ruin your horse.

One of the best ways to find a farrier is by recommendation, preferably by a veterinarian. Or, if you know of someone who has had horses for quite a while, he probably knows a good farrier. The only difficulty may be that that particular horseshoer is taking no new customers.

Finding a farrier on your own may be riskier, but if you are careful, you can reduce the potential problems. When you contact a farrier for the first time (many of them advertise in the newspaper, yellow pages, or in the local tack shop), find out what his schooling was. The days of apprenticeship are almost gone, and you will find that most of the qualified horseshoers are graduated from one of the recognized schools of farriery in the country.

First, find out how long he has been in business. Although experience is not an absolute criterion (there are plenty of farriers who have been doing things wrong for twenty years), it makes sense that, other considerations being equal, the farrier with the most experience is the best bet.

When the farrier you have chosen makes his first visit, be sure you are there. Also, have your horse ready. The farrier's time is valuable and he will either charge you extra for having to get your horse from the field, or refuse to do it at all. Have the horse's feet picked out and scrubbed. Be sure to provide a clean, dry, lighted area for the farrier to work in, and most important, be sure that the horse is accustomed to having each leg picked up and held. The farrier shoes horses—he doesn't train them. So if your horse is difficult, expect to be charged extra (if you're lucky enough to get him shod at all).

A good farrier keeps records of each horse he does—when it was last shod, condition of its feet, etc.—and may wish to observe your horse both standing and at a trot before he works on him.

A good farrier handles horses gently. He may punish a horse for being bad, but not for being frightened or ignorant. And he knows the difference.

The art of horseshoeing is a complex one, but a basic understanding of the principles is essential to every horse owner. There is an old axiom that horseshoeing is a necessary evil. This is not strictly true. First, it is not always necessary, and second, it is not always evil. The real evil, from the point of view of the horse, at least, is not the shoeing, but the riding. Nature made the horse to be a 20- to 25-mile-an-hour animal, equipped to jump easily over low obstacles, and to be able to run a mile or so at moderate speed without undue fatigue. He was not meant to carry weight, much less to race a mile and a quarter at blinding speed or jump over five-foot fences. But since mankind has adopted the horse for his own use, and put 150 pounds or more on his back, certain adaptations must be made. The major of these adaptations is shoeing.

The job of the farrier always begins with trimming the horse's hoofs, whether the horse is to be shod or not. This is not only the first part of the operation, but the most critical.

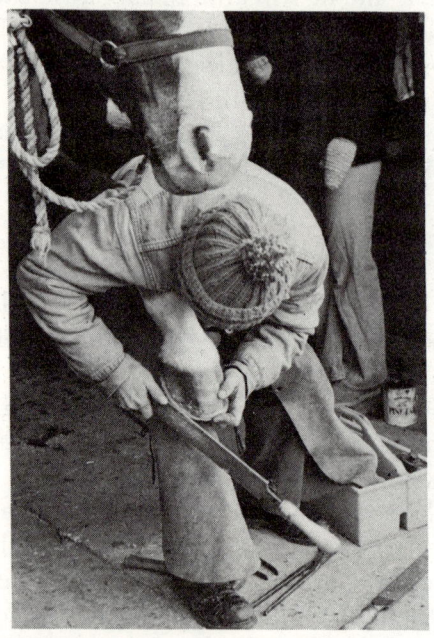

Farrier Lincoln Turner does some therapeutic shoeing on the horse shown on page 70. The temperature was near zero on this occasion; luckily he has a helpful owner assisting him here—also, to judge by the feet, some observers.

The finished job on the same horse.

If the hoof is not kept absolutely level and in balance, long-term damage may result. First the farrier will clean the hoof with his knife to remove loose flakes. Next he will nip off the excess hoof, taking care to keep the whole hoof, toe, heels, and quarters (sides) in balance. (This, by the way, does not mean that the length of the hoof wall must be equal down to the last centimeter. Forcing an animal's feet into unnatural symmetry may result in imbalance, rather than the opposite effect.)

Then the farrier will use the knife again, but sparingly. In the old days, farriers would often cut the frog completely out and trim the sole of the hoof so thin that it would yield on finger pressure. Even today some farriers will cut the bars before they do anything else. This is a disastrous mistake. The frog and sole, which are anti-concussion and shock absorbing devices, should be trimmed only enough to allow the proper set of the shoe. Removal of some of the dead, flaky material is necessary, but most of what is not needed for protection will slough off naturally anyway.

The bars of the hoof are supportive structures; they keep the heels open and allow the frog to function more effectively. They should be trimmed level with the walls, not cut back. To prevent corns, the sole should be lowered a bit between the walls and bars.

The final leveling of the hoof (done with a rasp) comes next. If the horse is not to be shod, the farrier will nip the toe in such a way as to make it easier for the animal to break over (page 51). He will leave the wall a quarter-inch longer than he would otherwise.

Horseshoes

The horseshoe serves several purposes. First of all, it protects the hoof, which is subjected to additional wear when the horse is ridden. Second, it provides traction for speed and safety, under certain conditions, on slippery surfaces. Third, it can be used to improve the gait of the horse or correct abnormal conditions of the foot and leg, such as contracted heels*, laminitis*, navicular trouble*, forging and bruising*. Fourth, it can alleviate the pain caused by certain conditions such as navicular trouble*.

Horseshoes are available in many different materials, such as iron, steel, aluminum (mostly for race horses), rubber, and plastic (a new development). Sometimes shoes are used in conjunction with pads of leather, felt, or plastic to further reduce concussion. It should be kept in mind, however, that the thick pads of gaited show horses in effect reduce the ground-bearing surface of the shoe at the heels and can thus increase strain.

Currently, there is a great deal of dissension among horseshoers and horseowners about the relative merits of "hot" and "cold" shoeing. In hot shoeing, the shoe is either handmade (an art in itself) or a "blank" is shaped after heating in a forge, then applied (warm, not hot) to the bottom of the hoof for proper fitting. In cold shoeing, the shoes (called keg shoes) are pre-sized and generally are made of more malleable material than in hot shoeing and can be completely shaped on the anvil. Hot shoeing is more versatile than cold shoeing, as some sorts of shoes cannot be bought and must be made by hand, but in the vast majority of cases, cold shoeing will do the trick. Many farriers do use both methods, but often prefer keg shoes, which come in nearly all sizes and shapes and save time and work. The real difference is not hot versus cold shoeing, but in the farrier. Although your horse is not Cinderella, the same principle applies: the shoe must fit the foot. Simple as this axiom is, however, it is amazing how often it is violated.

*An asterisk indicates a condition that is discussed in the Lamenesses section.

The shoe should be applied in such a way as to distribute concussion evenly. Only the weight-bearing sections of the hoof—that is, the walls and bars—should feel the pressure of the shoe. A common mistake is to rotate the shoe outward. Unfortunately, the resulting lameness may take months to develop, and so it may be difficult to accurately determine the true cause.

How can the owner be sure that his farrier is fitting the shoe properly? One clue, of course, is how much shaping he does on the shoe, particularly with cold shoeing. The chances that your horse's hoofs are exactly the same shape as the machine-made shoes is slight, and in most instances, three or four trips to the anvil must be made.

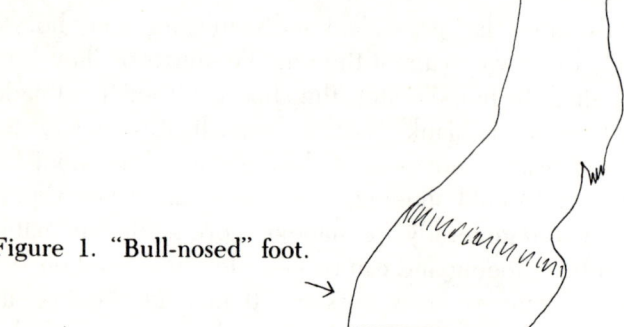

Figure 1. "Bull-nosed" foot.

Often there is a tendency for the shoe to be pulled towards the heel of the hoof as it is being nailed on; some farriers, instead of correcting this condition when it occurs, will simply file down the toe of the hoof. This is known as "cowboying" and the resulting hoof is called "bull-nosed." (Figure 1.)

The heels of the horseshoe should extend about one-quarter-inch behind the heel of the hoof, not so long that the horse is apt to pull it off, but long enough to cover the buttress of the hoof. Likewise the shoes should be slightly wider than the hoof at the quarters to allow for expansion. This is especially important for the front feet, which carry sixty percent of the weight of the horse and, further, are subject to a great deal more concussion than the hind feet.

After the shoe is properly fitted, it is nailed into place. Although keg shoes generally have eight nail holes, most farriers use only six or seven of them. For most hoofs, the rear nail holes are set too far back towards the heel of the hoof and, if used, would not allow for proper expansion of the foot. All the nails should be driven to approximately the same height, three-quarters of an inch above the shoe. Nails too high or too low can lead to extra hoof wall damage and make the shoe less secure. A nail driven too low or shallow causes splitting of the hoof wall, and high nails can be too close to the sensitive tissue (laminae). The nail should be driven into the "white line" of the hoof (the layer which separates the sensitive from the insensitive tissue) and emerge on the outside of the wall, where it is clinched. It sometimes happens, either because of farrier error or because of a peculiarity in the hoof structure, such as very straight walls, that the nail either pricks the sensitive tissue or is driven too close to it, a condition known as "nail bound." If this should happen, the nail must be pulled immediately and iodine poured into the hole, which should be widened with the hoof knife. A tetanus toxoid should then be given by a veterinarian.

As a finishing touch, some farriers rasp down the entire hoof wall to give it a neat appearance by removing the slight irregularities which occur in every normal hoof. Unfortunately, this practice also removes the varnish which covers and protects the hoof from drying, and should not be permitted. (Do not, though, confuse this with the filing underneath the horseshoe nails to allow for a better seating.)

Horseshoe additions, such as heel calks, toe grabs, and borium, are useful in certain instances, generally for better traction. On the whole, though, these additions interfere with the horse's natural gaits and can initiate lameness. Reducing the ground surface of the shoe subjects the hoof to increased concussion, which is a major factor in many lamenesses. Calks have even caused fractures of the long and short pastern bones by keeping the hoof stationary while the leg rotates. For this reason calks ought never be used on horses which are subjected to sudden turning, such as reining and roping animals. Borium increases the life of the shoe, prevents slipping on greasy surfaces, and adds traction, thus making it especially useful for parade, police, and endurance horses. But, like calks, it can subject your horse to added concussion, and in most cases is not at all necessary or desirable.

In addition to the above "normal" kinds of shoeing, there are also what are known as "corrective" and/or "therapeutic" shoeing. Although these terms overlap somewhat, and there is disagreement involving their meaning, in this book we shall consider "corrective" shoeing to refer to the artificial alteration of a horse's gaits for show purposes and "therapeutic" shoeing to indicate a method of shoeing which eliminates gait dysfunctions such as forging and interfering, or alleviates the discomfort brought on by certain hoof ailments such as navicular trouble, corns, or founder.

Corrective shoeing is largely accomplished by a combination of allowing the hoof to grow unnaturally long and by adding weights to the shoe. Weight at the toe causes the horse to reach out further with his legs than he would naturally, while heel weights cause him to lift his feet higher. Corrective shoeing is done mostly on gaited horses such as American Saddlebreds, Tennessee Walkers, and some Morgan show stock. The resulting action, while pleasing to some owners, reduces speed and greatly increases the fatigue of the horse, predisposing him to all sorts of lameness. The unnatural hoof length also increases strain on the ligaments and tendons, and in fact many of these otherwise lovely animals appear to be in chronic pain. Generally the long hoofs are accompanied by contracted heels due to the nonexistent frog pressure.

Therapeutic shoeing, on the other hand, is, as its name implies, a method of therapy. It attempts to restore a naturally balanced gait to an animal affected by poor conformation or disease. It makes use of roller shoes, bar shoes, pads, and other special aids. Therapeutic shoeing should, in general, be done gradually, and should not attempt to shape a horse's feet perfectly, but should attempt only to restore a balanced, *natural* foot as far as is possible.

According to many textbooks, for example, the ideal hoof angle for a front hoof is between 45 and 50 degrees and between 50 and 55 degrees for a hind hoof. In point of fact few hoofs possess this ideal angulation, mainly because the pastern and shoulder do not conform to it, and in most cases, hoof angle follows pastern and shoulder angle. This is how it should be. Forcing the hoof into an angle for which it is not naturally designed will only multiply the problems. If, however, the shoulder and pastern angle is not at fault, but the hoof itself is broken at the wrong angle, this can be corrected—gradually. If changes in angle of more than a few degrees are made at once, you run the risk of lameness due to strain on the tendons and ligaments.

CHAPTER 2

Your Horse

Q. "What is the prettiest side of the horse?"
A. "The outside."–OLD RIDDLE

Although the outside of the horse may be the nicest to look at, it's what's inside that counts. Your horse is a marvel of power, speed, and beauty, bones and muscle and articulations—wonderfully co-ordinated in an intricate design of movement. The owner should first understand the normal structure and function of the horse, so that he will be better able to understand lameness.

In considering the horse's body, we should begin with the bony framework, or skeleton. (Figure 2.) The skeleton, of course, is made up of bones; in the horse, 205 of them. Bones are living tissue and have blood vessels, nerves, and lymphatic vessels, and are subject to disease. They are composed of both organic and inorganic material; the former gives bones their resiliency and the latter their rigidity. Bone is incredibly strong—it has been estimated that its compressive strength is about 20,000 pounds per square inch. Bones are covered by a membrane, called the periosteum.

The function of the skeleton is to *support the body*. The horse's skeleton is classified as either *axial*, which consists mainly of the head and trunk, or *appendicular*, which pertains to the limbs. We will consider the axial skeleton briefly first.

Although there are 34 bones comprising the skull, they are all firmly joined together, with the exception, of course, of the lower jaw, or mandible.

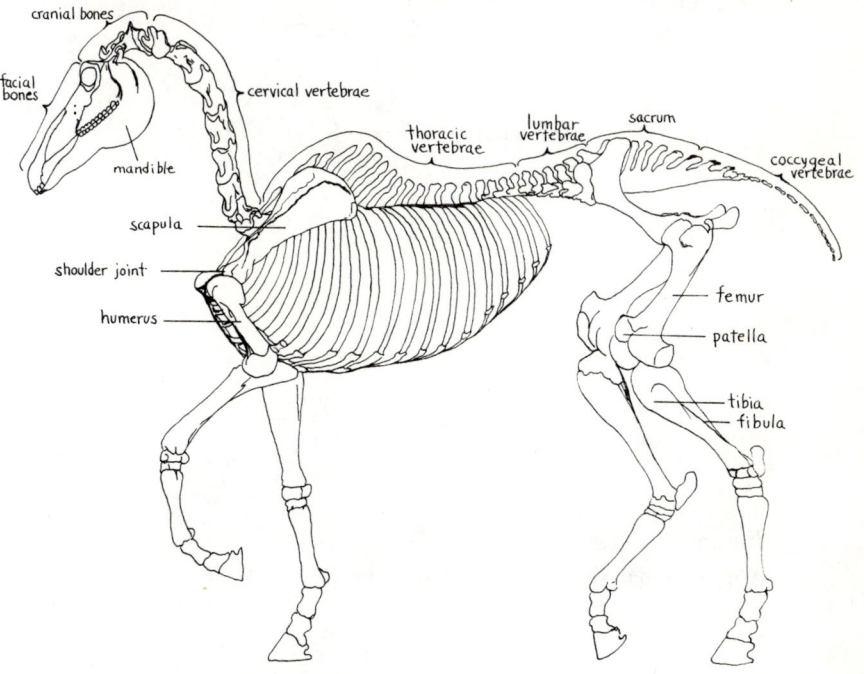

Figure 2. Skeleton of the horse.

The trunk is divided further into bones of the spinal column, the thorax, and the pelvis. The spinal column is the main support of the entire skeleton; it is made up of between 52 and 54 unpaired, odd-shaped vertebrae, which are placed in a long row from head to tail. Through them runs the spinal cord, the major nerve pathway for all the horse's movements.

The thorax consists of 18 pairs of ribs and the breast bone, or sternum, which is the base of the thorax. The sternum connects with the ribs and forms part of the chest cavity, in which are located the heart and lungs.

The pelvis is circular in shape and forms a prominent angle on the outside, which is known as the "point" of the hip.

However, it is the appendicular skeleton with which we are most concerned here. (Figure 3.)

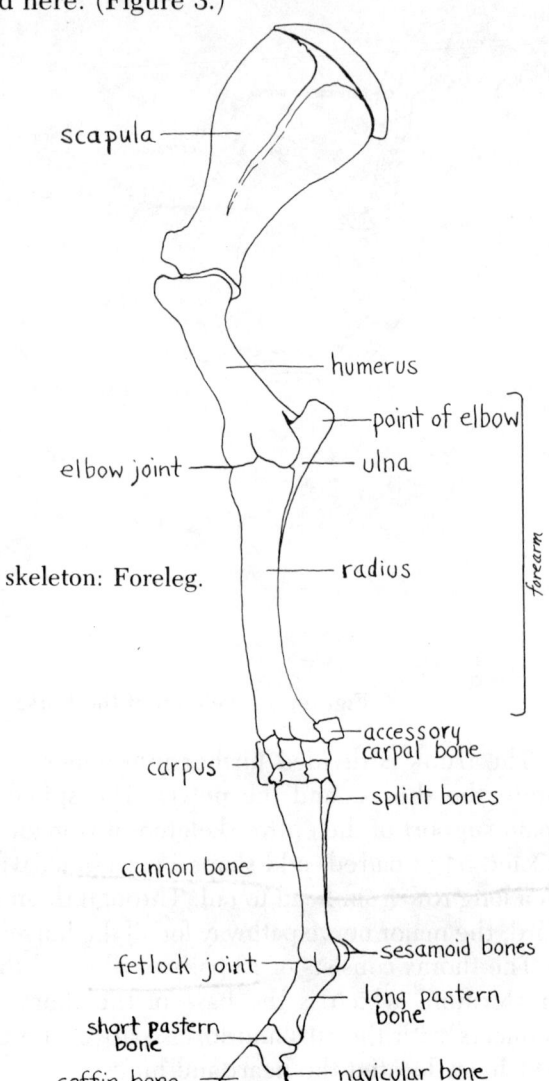

Figure 3.
Appendicular skeleton: Foreleg.

The Forelegs

The forelegs, which support over 60 percent of the horse's weight, are connected to the axial skeleton only by muscles. We will begin by looking at the most proximal (or highest) bone—the scapula, or shoulder blade. It is a large, flat, triangular-shaped bone, which lies on the side of the thorax. At its upper edge it is bordered by very elastic cartilages, and is connected only by muscles to the trunk. Ideally, it extends down and forward at an angle of 50 to 55 degrees. This angle is very desirable as a more upright shoulder tends to increase concussion. At its distal (lower) end the scapula articulates with the humerus or arm bone. The humerus is a fairly short bone which forms an angle of about 150 degrees with the fused bones of the elbow joint, the radius and ulna. The radius and ulna together form the forearm of the horse. The smaller, weaker ulna, partly fused to the radius in the full grown horse, lies behind it and projects to form the "point of elbow" or olecranon. This point forms a lever for the attachment of muscles which extend the elbow. In contrast to the humerus, the forearm should be long; this is essential to a long, flowing stride. The distal end of the radius articulates with the carpus, or knee. Actually, of course, the carpus is not a knee at all, but a wrist. If this seems rather peculiar, it is, but there you are: The knee is a wrist. At any rate, the carpus (which ideally should be nice and thick) consists of seven or eight bones arranged in two rows, and an accessory carpal bone to the rear, which does not actually bear weight.

Below the carpus is the cannon bone, or large metacarpal. The cannon bone is oval shaped, and flat in front. Its major function is to support weight, and it is put under incredible amounts of stress. It is surprising, and fortunate, that the cannon bone does not break oftener than it does. Ideally, the cannon bone should be short in relation to its distal fellow, the long pastern bone (or first phalanx), for this is the combination which produces greatest speed and least fatigue.

Attached to the cannon bone are two rudimentary metacarpals or "splint" bones. The splints are located one on each side and to the rear of the cannon bone, and are left over from the time when the horse had five toes like everyone else. The splints represent what are left of the "index" and "ring" fingers. (The other leftovers are the chestnuts which used to be thumbs and the ergots which used to be pinkies.) At the upper end, the splint bones form part of the bearing surface of the knee, and at the lower end are attached to the periosteum (or bone skin) of the cannon bone by ligaments which harden into bone, or ossify, by the time the horse is six years old.

The cannon bone and the long pastern bone form the fetlock joint, which is the most easily damaged joint in the horse's body, and will be giving us a good bit of trouble later on. For the time being we will pass it by.

The first phalanx corresponds to the first bone of the human middle finger. It is generally about one third the length of the cannon bone and extends downward and forward. Its function is to reduce concussion by increasing the flexibility of the fetlock joint. The pastern should slope at about the same angle as the shoulder—that is 50 to 55 degrees—and too much of a deviation is considered a conformation fault.

Also part of the worrisome fetlock joint are the two sesamoids (so called because of a supposed resemblance to sesame seeds), pyramid shaped bones located at the rear of the fetlock. These bones, which act as a fulcrum for some very important ligaments and tendons, are held in place by many small ligaments themselves. They are subjected to great stress and are often damaged, particularly in the high speed animal.

The short pastern, or second phalanx, attaches directly to the distal end of the long pastern, and is nearly a cube. It allows the foot to twist from side to side so that it can adjust to rough ground.

The short pastern connects to the coffin bone, which is

completely encased in the hoof. The coffin bone is very light and porous—simply filled with blood vessels—and, unhappily, is fractured rather easily. Wings of cartilage attach to the top and sides of the coffin bone and border a rubbery cushion which can be seen at bulbs of the heels. These are known as the lateral cartilage, which if they harden into bone, gives rise to a condition known as sidebone.*

At the rear of the coffin bone lies the navicular (or distal sesamoid) bone. It is small and oblong in shape—somewhat like a boat (hence its name). It has a ridge in the center, and a blunt end that lies behind and beneath the coffin joint. Like the proximal sesamoid bone, it acts as a fulcrum for the deep flexor tendon, which passes beneath it to attach to the coffin bone. The function of the navicular bone is to keep a constant angle of insertion for the deep flexor tendon. The navicular bone is covered with fibrocartilage on the side over which the deep flexor tendon passes. Held in place by many ligaments, its position between tendon and bone makes the navicular bone extremely vulnerable to crushing, bruising, and other injury.

The Hindlegs

The bones of the hindleg are reasonably analogous in most respects to those of the front. (Figure 4.)

The femur, or thigh bone, is the highest bone in the hindleg and is also the strongest. It points downward and forward and connects to the patella, the tibia, and the fibula to form the stifle joint. (This joint is prone to difficulties which we will consider later). The patella, or knee cap, glides over and articulates with the front of the distal end of the femur. The fibula, which is a small, thin bone corresponding to the ulna, lies against the upper and outer sides of the tibia, which articulates with the hock, or tarsus. The tarsus, or hock, corresponds to the carpus on the front leg. It consists of six small,

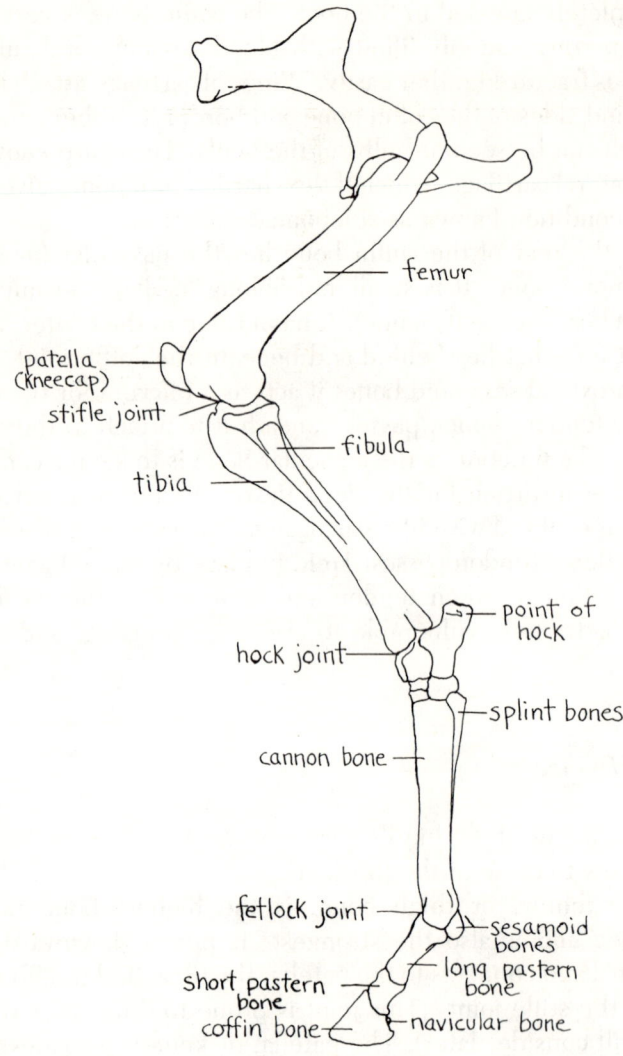

Figure 4. Appendicular skeleton: Hindleg.

irregular bones in three rows, one on top of another, and is formed by four joints. The so called "point of hock" is actually another bone, the calcanus (fibular tarsal bone), which projects behind the true hock joint, and is not really part of it. It acts as a lever for the muscles extending the hock.

Below the hock, the bones of the hind limb are exactly analogous to those in front, and have the same names.

All but the coffin bone (os pedis) are covered with a thin "periosteum" or bone skin. The periosteum provides for the increase in diameter of bones and helps to heal fractures.

All the bones of the horse contain small openings for blood vessels and nerves.

Blood Vessels and Nerves

Although the circulatory and nervous systems are not generally directly connected with lameness, every horseowner should have an elementary understanding of them as they apply to the leg.

Horses' blood, like that of humans, is a fluid which contains plasma, white and red cells, protein, simple sugars, electrolytes, and wastes of the body. It carries nutrients, oxygen, and hormones to the body tissues, and helps control temperature by transporting heat.

The blood is carried in three different types of blood vessels: arteries, capillaries, and veins. The arteries are tubular structures which carry blood directly from the heart to all parts of the body. Near each artery is a vein and nerves. Arteries are without valves and have thick elastic walls. If a horse has cut an artery, the blood will be bright red and will flow in spurts. A cut artery is extremely dangerous, since the horse can bleed to death in minutes. On either side of the pastern you may feel the digital artery as a light pulse, although the importance of this pulse is sometimes overrated as a diagnostic aid. In addition to the digital artery, and even more important for pulse taking, is the submandibular artery, found under the jaw.

When blood has passed from the arteries through the tiny capillaries of the foot it is taken back to the heart by the veins. This venous blood is darker than the arterial blood and flows in a steady stream. Veins are generally equipped with valves scattered at irregular intervals which aid the flow of blood to the heart. Compared to the arteries, blood pressure in the veins is quite low, and if a vein is cut, the blood will flow without spurting, and rather slowly. A cut vein is not so serious as a cut artery, since under normal conditions the blood will coagulate before too much of it is lost.

The whole foot contains a very extensive venous network, which many authorities feel aids in shock absorption by providing a kind of "suspension medium" that is compressed when the foot strikes the ground.

The nerves are round, white cords issuing from the brain and spinal cord. Generally they are quite close to the arteries. They subdivide until they are invisible to the naked eye. Injuries to the nerves may be permanent; cut nerves, for instance, may not grow back together, as skin will. However, if the damage to the nerves is caused by pressure, they may recover by themselves in time. Injuries to the nerves can be caused by cuts, crushing, poison, infections, and tumors.

CHAPTER 3

Joints, Tendons, Muscles, and Ligaments (The Ties that Bind)

JOINTS

The joints (technically known as *articulations*) are located at the meeting of two or more bones. Joints have two major functions: first, they bear weight, and second, they allow for movement. At the ends of the bones, where they meet, there is generally one convex surface (the head or *condyle*) and one concave (*glenoid* or *cotyloid*) surface. Both these surfaces are covered with an elastic cartilage.

There are three sorts of joints: movable, slightly movable, and immovable. The immovable articulations, also called *sutures*, are found mostly in the head. Of the movable joints, those which allow complete freedom of movement are called *synovial*, or free joints. These are most important for the movement of the horse. Examples are the joints of the shoulder and hip. Other joints, such as the fetlock, hock, and elbow permit motion in two directions only, flexion and extension. These are known as *hinge* joints. All the joints are enclosed by air-tight *capsular ligaments*, the inside of which form the synovial membrane. This important and delicate membrane produces the synovial fluid, or joint oil. Synovial fluid lubri-

JOINTS, TENDONS, MUSCLES, LIGAMENTS

cates the joint and reduces friction. It is light yellow, viscous, transparent, and contains protein. The joint capsules are surrounded by *annular* ligaments, which protect them.

TENDONS

We cannot consider the joints in isolation, for they are literally bound up with the ligaments (which connect bone to bone) and the tendons (which join bone to muscle). In general, we can say that the function of the tendons is to translate the movement of the muscles to the bones. The tendons move

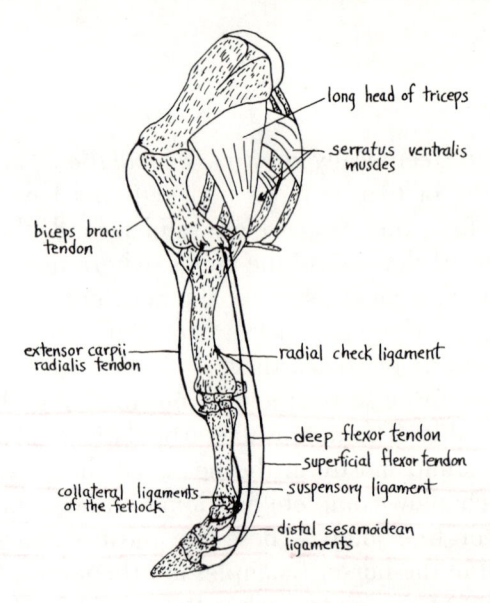

Figure 5. Major ligaments and tendons of the forelimb.

in loose, lubricated sheaths (composed of two layers of synovia, which secrete synovial fluid) and are themselves usually inelastic. The elasticity needed to produce fluid motion is provided by the muscles to which they are attached. (The horse has no muscles *per se* below the knee.)

The tendons, which are an integral part of the horse's movement system, are of two types—extensors and flexors. The extensors, which straighten the leg, are located in the anterior (front) part of the foreleg, and the flexors, which flex or bend the leg, are located in the posterior (back) part.

The main extensor tendon runs down the front of the leg, and connects to the first phalanx, second phalanx, and coffin bone, or third phalanx. As its name implies, this broad tendon extends the leg when the muscle to which it is connected contracts. Parallel to the main extensor tendon runs the lateral extensor tendon, which attaches on the outside of the first phalanx at its upper end. This tendon is present in the hind leg too, where it attaches to the point of hock, but in that location it flexes the leg.

In the back of the front leg, there are two *flexor tendons* which attach to the phalanges. One is the superficial flexor tendon, which lies right under the skin. It is easily felt and has the tautness of a drawn bow when the horse is putting weight on the foot. It passes down the back of the leg and divides below the fetlock. It acts simultaneously on both phalanges by attaching to the lower end of the second phalanx. When it reaches the sesamoid bone, it loops around its companion, the deep flexor tendon. The sesamoid bones act like a fulcrum for it. The superficial flexor tendon acts like a ligament, in that there is a little muscle tissue left in it, and it functions mainly as a part of the stay apparatus.

The deep flexor tendon is cylindrical in shape, and is somewhat longer than the superficial flexor. It lies directly behind the latter and shares the same tendon sheath. It attaches to the coffin bone, where a fulcrum is formed by the navicular bone.

Wherever tendons must pass over these lumpy bones, there are mucous bursae to protect them.

MUSCLES

A muscle is a bundle of fibers, which contract to originate movement. There are three sorts of muscle: smooth muscle, cardiac muscle, and skeletal muscle. It is skeletal muscle which is responsible for movement and with which we are concerned here. A muscle, when not fatigued, can generally contract almost half the length of its fibers. However, when the muscle does become tired, it is unable to contract so quickly or completely, and more strain is placed upon the inelastic tendon. This, in brief, is why tendons bow.

LIGAMENTS

The ligaments, which, as we said, connect bone to bone, are more elastic than tendons. Their function primarily is to support weight.

The ligaments are of three basic kinds. First, the "binding" ligaments, which hold the bones together; second, the check ligaments, which hold the tendons to the bone and help prevent muscle strain; and third, the capsular ligaments, which secrete and contain the synovial fluid. Ligaments vary in color from white to yellow—the more yellow, the more elastic.

The most important ligament, for the horse owner, is the wide, powerful suspensory ligament, also called the interosseous muscle. The suspensory ligament originates partly at the lower row of carpal bones (or tarsals, in the hind leg) and partly at the upper end of the cannon bone between the two heads of the splint bones. It divides about two thirds of the way down the cannon bone (just above the nodules of the splint bones) into two branches, each one of which is attached to a sesamoid bone, where it divides again and attaches at the top and sides. Somewhat elastic, the suspensory ligament

JOINTS, TENDONS, MUSCLES, LIGAMENTS 39

supports the fetlock and prevents it from dorsiflexing, or extending too far.

THE STAY APPARATUS

Both the tendons and the ligaments help to operate what is known as the "stay apparatus" of the horse. (Figure 6.) This is a complex, flexible system of tendons and ligaments that, in short, keeps the horse standing—and explains why he can sleep in this position.

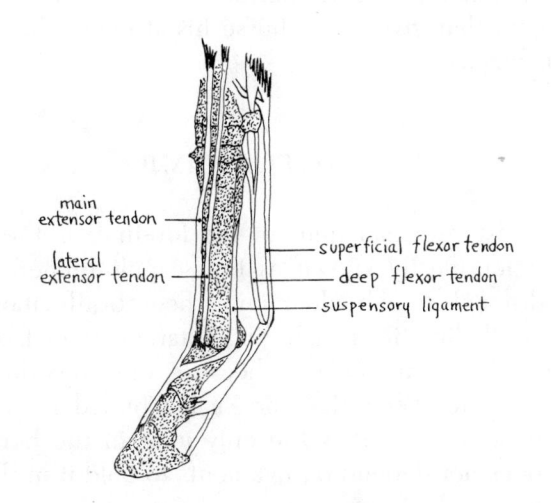

Figure 6. System of "stay apparatus" of the forelimb.

What the stay apparatus actually does is to support the leg, reduce concussion, and prevent overextension of the fetlock. When the horse is at rest, his weight is supported by strong bands of connective tissue. Connective tissue joins other tissues together and supplies strength and protection to them. Ligaments, tendons, and cartilage are examples of connective tissue. In the forelegs the stay apparatus contains many components, the intersesamoidean ligament, the collateral sesamoidean ligament, the suspensory ligament, the distal sesamoidean ligament (which binds the sesamoid bones to the phalanx), the short sesamoidean ligaments, the collateral ligaments of the fetlock, the serratus ventralis muscles, the biceps brachii tendon, the extensor carpi radialis tendon, the long head of the triceps muscle, the superior or radial check ligament, and the deep flexor tendon. It is certainly not necessary to remember all these names, or even to understand exactly how the system works. It is important to know, however, that it is this wonderful system of pulleys, fulcrums, and levers that gives your horse his strength, his elasticity, and his beauty.

THE FORELIMB

The most proximal joint of the forelimb is the shoulder joint—scientifically known as the scapulo-humeral articulation. Although the shoulder joint theoretically allows movement in all directions including rotation, it in fact permits little extension and flexion, because the powerful pectoral (chest) muscles keep the horse's leg pulled in toward the body, or adducted. It is the only joint in the horse's body which does not depend on ligaments to hold it in the correct position.

The humerus connects with the radius and ulna to form the elbow joint. The elbow joint has two positions only—open and closed—hence it is a true hinge joint.

The knee joint really consists of three separate joints in two rows of bones—the radial carpal, the intercarpal, and the carpal-metacarpal. When the horse bends his knee, the bones of the radial carpal and intercarpal joints separate in front while remaining in contact behind. Each row of joints is capsuled in a synovial sac. At the back of the knee is a large "sesamoid" bone, the accessory carpal, which does not bear weight. The carpal bones are able to move in several directions when weight is placed on them, and are quite resilient and springy. They aid greatly in the reduction of concussion. This whole structure is bound together with numerous ligaments, which unfortunately are frequently damaged.

The fetlock, or metacarpo-phalangeal articulation (now there's a word for you), is a true hinge joint, and moves considerably when made to bear weight. It can move in two directions only, forward and backward; that is, it flexes and extends. It is supported by many ligaments—the sesamoid ligaments and the intersesamoid ligament which ties the two sesamoid bones together.

The fetlock, being far from the center of rotation of the limb, has considerable pressure exerted on it, and is often damaged.

The coronary of the pastern joint, where the first and second phalanx meet, is a simple joint, somewhat limited in motion. It has eight ligaments beside the capsular one.

The coffin, or pedal joint, is an imperfect hinge joint which allows quite a bit of side to side (lateral) movement.

THE HINDLIMB

The most proximal joint of the hindlimb is the sacro-iliac joint, a joint with very limited movement and small importance as far as lameness is concerned.

The hip joint is a ball-and-socket joint which, like the shoulder, theoretically permits movement in all directions, but which in fact is pretty well limited to flexion and extension.

The stifle joint, which becomes rigid when the horse places his foot on the ground, is an important force-resisting structure. It is really made up of two joints, the femoropatellar and the femorotibial. The stifle flexes and extends with a very small amount of axial rotation. In a normal standing position its angle is about 150 degrees.

The hock forms the center of the major movements of the hind foot. The hock and the stifle *must work together*. If one is flexed the other must be flexed also. The most important hock joint, the tibiotarsal, is formed by the tibia and the cannon and splint bones. Composed of six bones, it does not permit as much movement as its counterpart the knee. Full extension is prevented by the collateral ligaments. The main articulation occurs at the tibiotarsal joint—all the other joints are restricted by ligaments to sliding. In normal standing position the angle formed is about fifty degrees. One very important ligament is the *plantar* ligament at the rear of the hock. It runs from the point of hock to the upper end of the cannon bone and acts as a brace.

CHAPTER 4

Anatomy and Physiology of the Foot

The words "hoof" and "foot," although overlapping in definition, have somewhat distinctive meanings. "Hoof" (figures 7 and 8) refers to the epidermus, or outside layer of the foot. It includes the wall, sole, and frog. The hoof itself is nonvascular; that is, it has no blood vessels or nerves. This explains why it does not hurt the horse to have nails driven into the hoof. It is often said to be "cornified," which simply means that it is hornlike in structure, and indeed, like the rhino's horn, is really made up of modified hair fibers.

The foot itself includes the hoof and all the structures within it, such as the corium, which provides the vascular and nerve supply, the digital cushion, ligaments and tendons, and sensitive structures.

The hoof wall, which supports the weight of the horse, grows about one-third to one-half an inch a month, depending on nutrition, moisture, temperature, and the activity of the horse. Since the part of the wall at the heels has a shorter distance to grow, the wall is younger there and more elastic than at the toe. The wall is thickest at the toe, also, and thins toward the heels. The wall functions to resist wear, act as a shock absorber, and provide traction. Generally speaking, you may find that dark colored hoofs are much tougher and less brittle than white or unpigmented ones.

44   ANATOMY AND PHYSIOLOGY

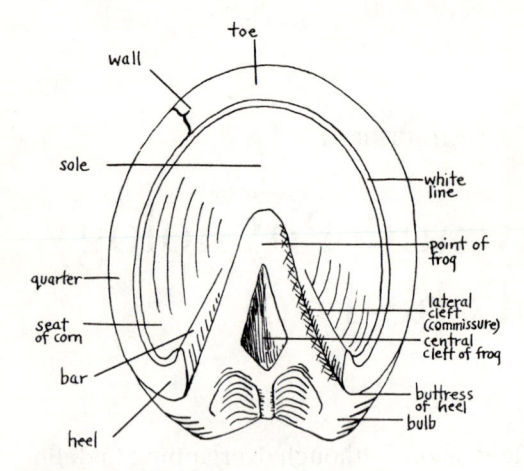

Figure 7. Hoof: Bottom aspect.

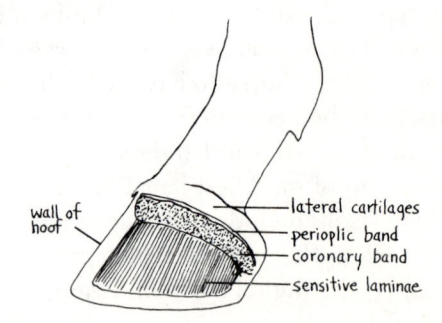

Figure 8. Internal structure of foot (hoof wall removed).

The outside of the wall is covered with a natural waxy hoof varnish, or perioplic layer (stratum tectorium), which will help prevent moisture from leaking out of the hoof. It is produced by the narrow perioplic band, which is located just above the coronary band and helps protect it. The fibrofatty coronary band is the major source for hoof wall nutrition and growth. (Those wavy lines you may see around your horse's hoofs reflect variations in feed, health, and temperature.) Located at the very top of the foot and pliable in texture, the coronary band is composed of tiny papillae which are filled with blood vessels. The papillae are fingerlike structures which lock into the horn tubules of the hoof wall. If the coronary band should be injured, it may mean defective hoof wall growth below that area.

The wall itself is about 25 percent water. It is arranged in thick-walled rigid tubules of various diameters which run from the coronary band to the ground. These tubules are cemented together by a substance called intertubular horn. The horn tubules themselves are filled with loosely packed cells which are responsible for the conduction of water.

The triangular piece of tissue you see at the bottom of the hoof is the frog. This is a tough protector of the sensitive structure it covers. Fifty percent of the frog is composed of water, a fact which largely accounts for its resiliency. This horny or non-sensitive frog is somewhat different from the other horny structures in that it is not completely turned to solid horn; thus it is more elastic. Fat-secreting glands, akin to human sweat glands, extruding a greasy fluid, help keep the frog pliable. It is thought that the frog acts like an assistant pump, to help keep the blood flowing back up the leg.

At the ground surface, the wall turns in to form the bars, which are very tough, and help support weight.

The hard "floor" of the hoof is called, sensibly enough, the sole. Like the wall it is made up of horn tubules. It is naturally about three-eighths to one-quarter inch thick at the heel. The insensitive sole acts as a protection for the sensitive sole beneath, which nourishes it. This sensitive sole can be easily bruised, particularly if the horny sole is pared too thin by the farrier. On the other hand, some horses retain an unnaturally thick sole. This is known as a "false sole" and can be an indication of disease.

The innermost layer of the hoof wall is called the laminar layer, which partly acts to increase the surface area of weight support. If you scrub your horse's hoof, you will notice the *white line* which indicates the true shape of your horse's foot. It is here that the sensitive laminae interlock with the horny structures of the wall by means of many tiny "primary papillae" or fingerlike projections.

All the sensitive tissues of the hoof are well supplied with blood from the digital arteries. Lymph vessels are also plentiful in the laminae. When weight is put on the hoof, the vessels of the sensitive structures are compressed between the horny structures and the coffin bone.

As there are no valves in the veins of the foot itself, the blood there can flow in either direction. The compression of the veins by the digital cushion or hoof against the lateral cartilages acts like a pump to push the blood back up the leg toward the heart. The veins in the leg are provided with valves to keep the blood from flowing backward.

Another cushioning device of the foot is the so-called "bulb," or digital (plantar) cushion, found in the rear half of the foot. This wedgelike structure has few blood vessels and nerves but a great deal of fibro-elastic, fatty material containing cartilage. It acts mainly as a shock absorber.

On the sides of the digital cushion are the lateral cartilages, winglike structures attached to the coffin bone. About one-half of the lateral cartilage is confined within the hoof—the rest extends above the coronet. Like the digital cushion it is very elastic, and probably serves to reduce concussion and aid in blood circulation. The lateral cartilages are partly fibrous in structure and partly hyaline (clear) cartilage.

It is important to remember that the horse's foot is not a simple structure, but a *system*. Each element in the system has a job to do—support weight, reduce concussion, or pump blood. If any structure in the foot is injured or not working well, because of poor nutrition, poor shoeing, or poor riding practices, the effects will soon show up elsewhere. And eventually your horse will become lame.

CHAPTER 5

Hoof Care

Although the mechanism of the foot appears to be complex and somewhat delicate, good hoof care is not a particularly difficult task. We have already discussed shoeing, and proper riding and training should be largely a matter of common sense. Two factors are of paramount importance—cleanliness and proper moisture control. Both of these factors can be controlled by the owner.

A common problem is dry or brittle hoofs. Although this tends to occur most often in horses with white, unpigmented feet, all horses are subject. Brittle feet can be caused by a long spell of dry weather, especially in combination with rocky soil and moisture absorbant bedding such as sawdust or wood shavings. The remedy is simple; until the drying conditions are altered, treat the hoofs daily with lanolin, pine tar, olive oil, or any good commercial hoof dressing. It is important to moisten the feet before applying the dressing, since the agent will lock in (or out) whatever moisture is present. (Do not use motor or mineral oil, however; these oils will close the pores of the horn and will increase the problem.)

Remember that the horn in both sole and wall absorb and yield moisture readily.

Too dry hoofs are a more serious problem in a horse that is to be shod, since the nails will tend to crack the horn in such cases. Barefoot horses tend to develop somewhat drier feet in any event, as this gives them a little added protection on hard surfaces. If the hoof remained too soft it would wear away quickly.

Too moist feet can create their own problems. This condition develops when a horse is left for too long in a damp pasture, or it can result from too zealous application of moisturizing agents. The over-moist foot, like the over-dry foot, lacks resiliency and spring. In such a state the major anti-concussion device of the horse is rendered ineffective, and a host of lamenesses can result because the foot becomes too easily permeated by microbes that thrive in moisture.

The role of cleanliness in proper hoof care cannot be overemphasized. Filth is the primary cause of both thrush and canker and a contributing cause to several other hoof ailments. Not only should the horse's hoofs be picked daily, but his bedding should be changed frequently, and his stall limed periodically.

CHAPTER 6

Equine Locomotion

Before considering conformation defects and lameness, the horseowner should understand basically what is involved when the horse moves.

Locomotion simply means the act of moving from one place to another. To do this successfully the horse must (a) shift his center of gravity from one point to another, and (b) keep from falling down while doing it. This may sound easy, but each leg has a variety of jobs to do—push and pull, maintain balance, support weight, and effect recovery after each stride. And of course it is essential that each leg not get tangled up with the others while doing it!

It is important to remember that the forelimbs of the horse are attached to the axial skeleton only by muscles and skin. When the horse is standing squarely on all four legs, the front limbs, from the elbow down, are completely locked. To generate the first step in forward motion in the front legs, the brachicephalis muscle pulls the leg forward, or protracts it. Simultaneously the large serratus thoracis muscle, which looks somewhat like a fan, contracts. This, by the way, is a primary principle in body movement, known as reciprocal muscle action. When one muscle contracts, another muscle must relax.

In the rear leg, it is the iliopsoas muscle that protracts the leg, which is brought back by the gluteus medias and hamstrings. The hock is opened by the gastrocnemius muscle which connects the point of hock with an attachment above the stifle. In general, the hind limbs are designed to drive the body forward, while the forelimbs lift as well as push. The forelimbs also act as the main brakes.

As the horse starts to pull his front leg forward, it bends at the knee, to reduce fatigue. Then, as the forearm extends fully, the extensor carpi radialis straightens the carpus again. As the foot strikes the ground, the body continues to push forward while the leg is already moving back. At this point, the foreleg supports the weight of the horse. It is prevented from moving any further backward by the suspensory ligament and both flexor tendons. (Figure 9.) They resist overflex-

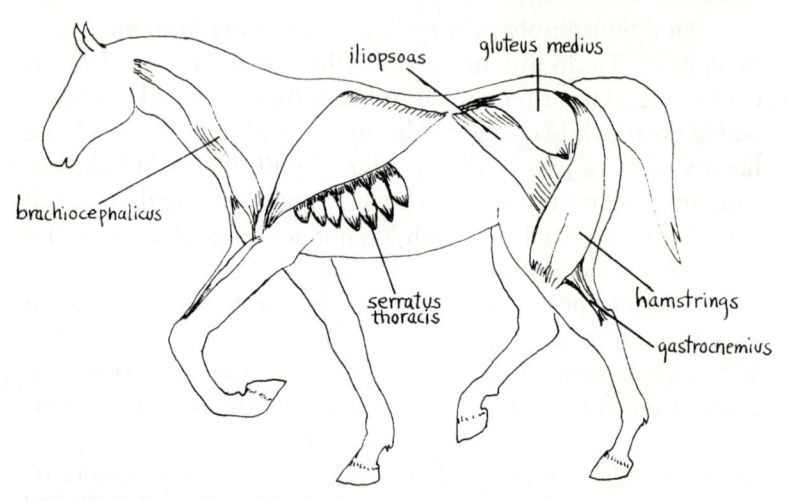

Figure 9. Muscles of horse locomotion.

ion of the fetlock and coffin joints. As the forelimbs take weight, the elbow joint locks and the whole leg becomes a rigid column. It is now that the body of the horse is propelled forward. During the recovery phase of the stride, the limb is pulled forward and then bent so as to clear the ground. It is then pushed forward and the cycle of protraction, retraction and support begins again.

The front end of the horse, which receives most of the concussive force, is doubly taxed when jumping. In that instance the entire weight of the animal is absorbed through one foot. The second foot, although receiving not so great a shock as the first, lands in such a position that the tendons are strained and squeeze tightly against the navicular bone. This is one reason why jumping horses in particular are prone to navicular problems.

Proper riding technique, such as that taught in dressage training, can develop rhythm and cadence in your horse; undue strain will be lessened or eliminated and you will find yourself with a freer moving, healthier, and happier horse.

GAITS

The word "gait" signifies a particular pattern of motion, occurring in a series of strides. A stride refers to the completed action of a single limb.

In horses, the height, length, and formation of the stride is influenced by two things—(1) the conformation of the horse and (2) the length of the toe.

As far as conformation is concerned, a major factor to note is the point at which the foot "breaks over." (Figure 10.)

Figure 10. Ideal point of breakover.

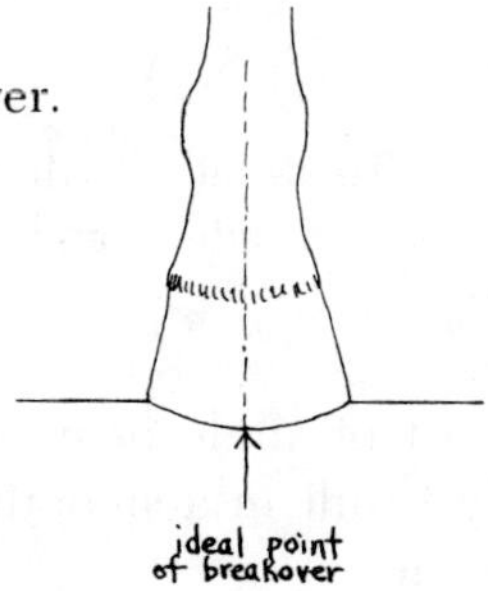

Breakover refers to the point at which the foot begins to roll forward in its transition from ground to air. This largely determines the "flight path" each foot will take. To travel in a straight line, the foot must break over at the center of the toe. If the foot must break over toward the inside of the toe (figure 11a), however, which often occurs with "toed-out" horses, the foot will move in an inward arc. This is known as "winging-in." If the foot breaks over to the outside (figure 11b), as occurs in many "toed-out" horses, the foot will travel in the outward arc; this is known as "paddling."

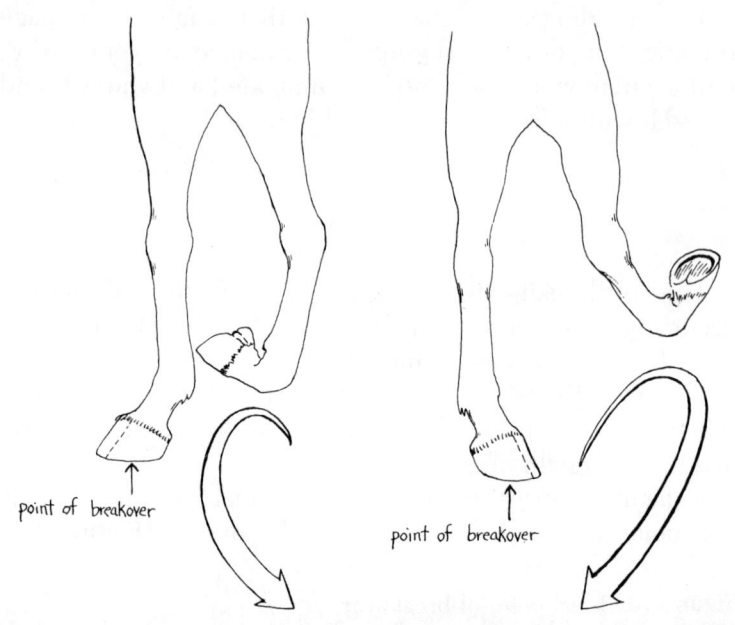

Figure 11a. "Toed-out" with breakover on inside and "winging-in."

Figure 11b. "Toed-in" with breakover on outside and "paddling."

A pastern-foot angle near the ideal 50 degrees (figure 12) will usually result in a smooth, round, vertical arc, which is what you want.

Figure 12. Pastern-foot angles.

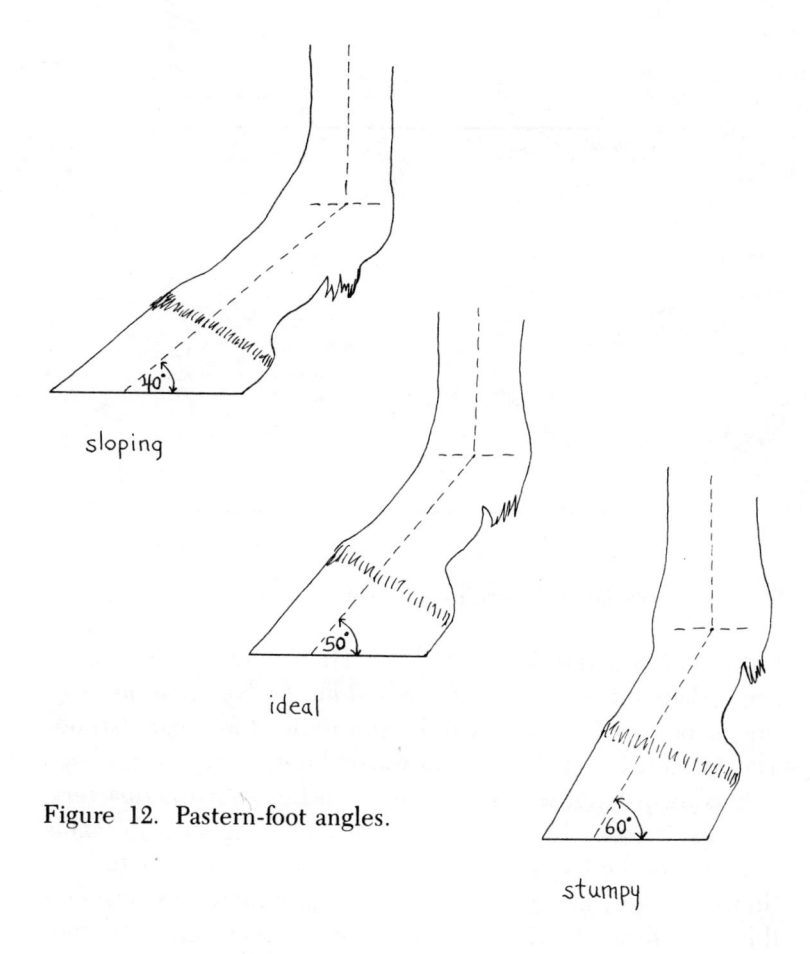

sloping

ideal

stumpy

An angle greater than about 50 degrees will result in a quicker breakover and a higher, shorter stride. An angle less than 45 degrees results in a slower breakover and a longer, lower flight path (figure 13).

To counteract or enhance the natural stride of the horse, some farriers will alter the relative toe and heel lengths of the hoofs. A toe which is left short breaks over quickly and puts

54   EQUINE LOCOMOTION

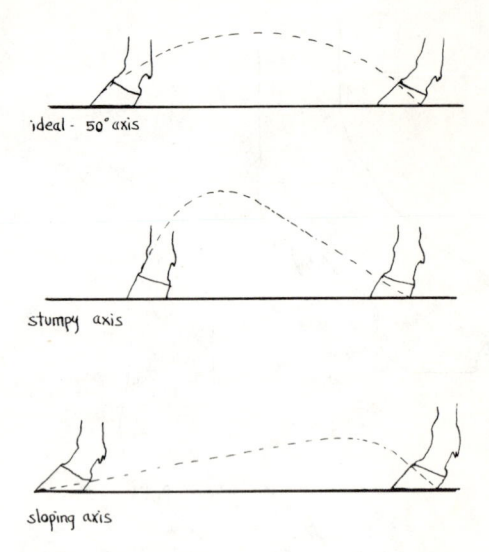

ideal - 50° axis

stumpy axis

sloping axis

Figure 13. Variation in strides from different pastern-foot angles.

little strain on the flexor tendons. However, if this practice contradicts the *natural angle formed by the hoof and pastern*, the suspensory ligament will be put under too great a strain. This is known as a "broken forward" hoof (figure 14a).

Raising or lengthening the toe (or paring away the quarters) will result in a "broken-back" hoof angle (figure 14b). This shoeing method is sometimes applied to racehorses to give them a longer, lower stride, but it greatly increases strain on the deep flexor tendon. It also tends to create great fatigue, owing to the slower breakover.

The gaits of the horse may be divided into the symmetrical and the asymmetrical. Symmetrical gaits are balanced gaits; that is, opposite legs correspond in movement, and the strain on the horse is greatly reduced.

The most easily understood of the symmetrical gaits is the trot (figure 15a), which is also known as a diagonal support gait. In the *true trot*, the left hindfoot and the right forefoot

EQUINE LOCOMOTION 55

strike the ground simultaneously, as do the right hind and left fore. At any given moment there are either two or no feet on the ground. Equilibrium is easy to obtain at this gait, as the horse is perfectly balanced all around. The length of the stride at the trot ranges from about nine feet for the average saddle horse to seventeen or more for a Thoroughbred.

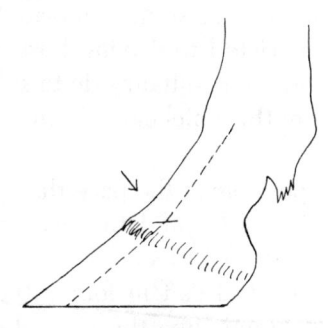

Figure 14a. "Broken-back" hoof angle

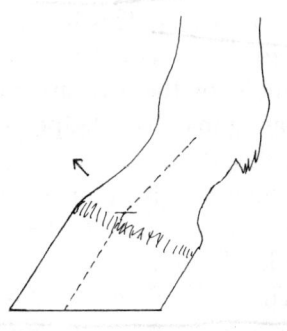

Figure 14b. "Broken-forward" hoof angle.

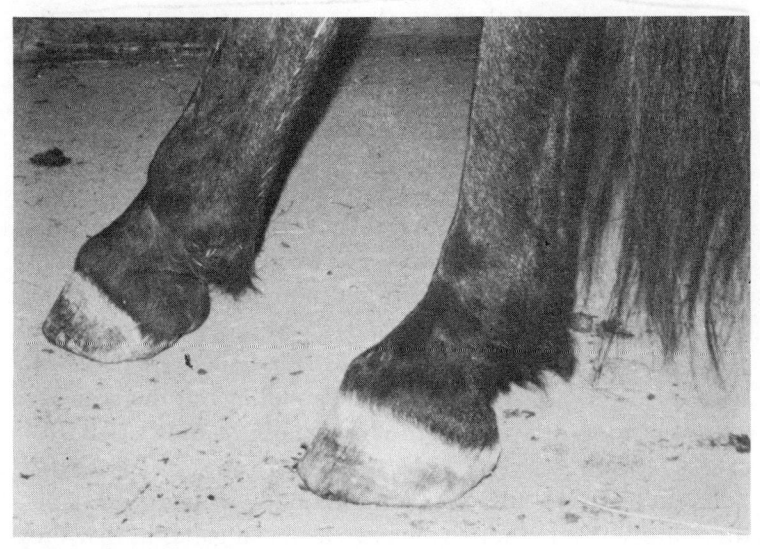

Broken forward axis.

Allied to the trot is the *pace* (figure 15b), a lateral-support gait. At this gait the horse moves first his left, then his right feet in unison. Like the trot, then, this is a two-beat gait, with a period of suspension when no feet are touching the ground. Support is a little more precarious at this gait, however, since the horse must shift his center of gravity from side to side as he progresses. This is what makes the pace so uncomfortable to ride, and why it is generally restricted to driving horses. Camels, by the way, are pacers, and the resultant side to side swaying may have helped earn them their nickname "ships of the desert."

Theoretically, a longer stride is possible at the pace than at the trot, as opposite legs won't interfere, and the average stride of the Standardbred pacer is 12 to 14 feet.

The walk (figure 15c) is a symmetrical gait in four rather than two beats. This sequence is lateral, like the pace, because both feet of one side strike the ground before the feet of the opposite side. The hoofbeats are all separate, though, and evenly spaced, and there is always at least one foot on the ground at all times. Since this gait has both continuous support and steady impulsion, it is the "locomotion of choice" as far as ease and comfort to the horse are concerned. The average length of the stride is approximately six feet.

The Tennessee Walking Horse has a variation on the normal walk, called the "running walk." At this gait, at which the horse moves six to eight miles per hour, the hind foot oversteps the front by up to a yard. Although it is a comfortable gait for the horse in most respects, the energy required to move all four legs in different ways simultaneously (and with speed) along with the necessary "straddling" of the rear legs (so as not to interfere with the front limbs) seems an effort in excess of the result.

In addition to the above-mentioned symmetrical gaits, there are several others which are artificial gaits, in that they have to be taught to the horse.

EQUINE LOCOMOTION

These include the "fox-trot"—a sort of cross between the walk and the trot in four beats. The pace is usually quite slow, proceeding left rear, right fore, right rear, and left fore, with the horse's head nodding in rhythm to the movement.

The "stepping-pace" is a slow, highly collected gait performed by the Five Gaited American Saddlebred. It is a

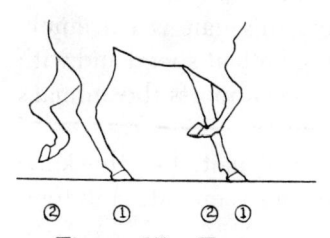

Figure 15a. Trot.

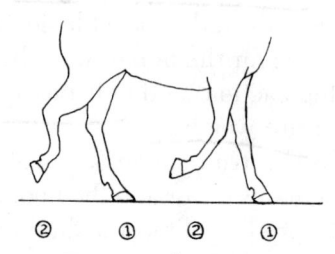

Figure 15b. Pace.

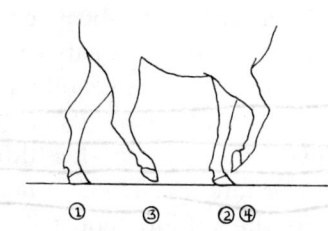

Figure 15c. Walk.

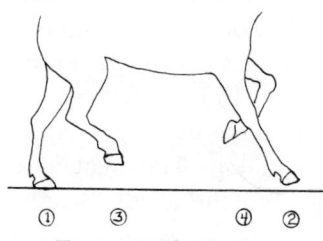

Figure 15d. Rack.

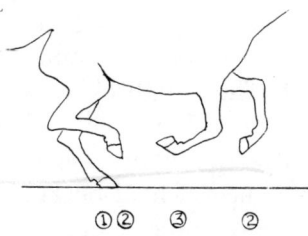

Figure 15e. Gallop.

four-beat lateral gait in the sequence right rear, right fore, left rear, left fore.

The rack—sometimes inaccurately known as the "singlefoot" (figure 15d)—is the speed gait of the American Saddlebred. Like the stepping pace, which immediately precedes it in the show ring, it is a four-beat gait—left rear, right fore, right rear, left fore. Although a brilliant gait and both smooth and enjoyable for the rider, this gait is extremely tiring for the horse, since he is moving both at speed and with high action, and only one hoof at a time supports the animal's entire weight.

The true singlefoot is also a four-beat gait, but the knee action is lower and the hoof beats are not so separate, but tend to produce almost a shuffling gait.

The horse possesses one primary asymmetrical gait—the gallop (figure 15e). In an asymmetrical gait, the axial skeleton tends to bend and the spacing between the hoof beats is uneven. The gallop is a fast three-beat gait. (When the Thoroughbred is at a flat run, four beats can sometimes be heard.) In the gallop, the horse pushes off with one hind leg (first beat), then the other hind leg and its diagonal fore fellow (second beat), and finally the other foreleg (third beat), which lands in front of the first fore leg. This last hoof indicates the "lead." If, for example, the left fore foot strikes the ground in front of the right, the horse is said to be on the left lead. This gait has the effect of powerfully thrusting the body forward. The *rhythm*, but not the speed, of the gait is fairly slow so that the horse is able to gather all his muscles for the next bound. This is one of the reasons why he can attain great speed at this gait. The length of the stride is between 15 and 22 feet, although a Thoroughbred can achieve a markedly longer one.

The canter or lope is a restrained gallop. The beat and sequence of hoof beats are the same, but the stride is only about ten or 12 feet.

CHAPTER 7

Conformation

Conformation indicates the relationship between form and function. A horse with good conformation performs well and stays healthy; a horse with poor conformation is apt to be stiff, uncomfortable to ride, and, more often than not, eventually lame. This is because conformation is the key to the horse's movement.

When considering the conformation of the horse, it is wise to begin at the hoof—in obedience to the old maxim "no hoof, no horse"—and then work up. That way you can be sure you haven't missed anything. After you have determined the quality of each individual structure, you can then proceed to examine the relationship *between* the structures.

THE HOOF (Figure 16)

Most people, when prospecting for a horse, look at the head before they do anything else; what is worse, they allow their impressions of the head to color their attitude towards the rest of the horse. This is an error. The horse, after all, does not walk on its head. Many a strong, sound horse has been by-passed because of an unfortunate nose, and many an anatomical wreck has been bought because of a fine head. Let's, then, start at the bottom, the hoof.

CONFORMATION

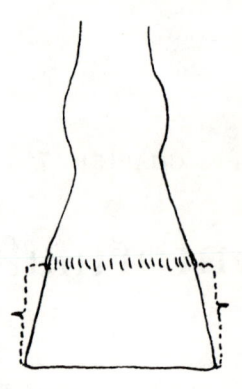

Figure 16. Ideal hoof: Distance from ground to coronary band should be the same on both sides.

The size of the hoof should be proportionate to the size of the horse. Too-small hoofs, which are all too common with some strains of the Quarter Horse, are inadequate to support the weight of the horse, and too-large ones tend to make him clumsy.

Examine the hoof carefully from the front. It is essential that the hoof be balanced; that is, the coronary band should be no farther from the ground to the inside of the hoof than it is to the outside. One hoof wall may be longer than the other, but the distance from ground surface to coronary band should be the same.

The hoof wall should be smooth, straight, and free from cracks. Many or extremely wavy lines could indicate a history of disease. The front feet will be more rounded and slightly flatter than the hind hoofs, due to greater concussion. Normally, the outside half of the hoof will be fuller and have more slant. The frog ought to be fairly large, and maintain contact with the ground. If the frog does not touch the ground, it cannot act as a shock absorber and auxiliary blood pump, the purposes it was designed for. The frog should also be free of evidence of disease such as thrush (which makes its presence known by its foul smell). The heels should be well open—

CONFORMATION 61

approximately one quarter of the circumference of the whole hoof.

The sole should have a good dome, and the whole texture of the hoof should be tough, but not dry or brittle.

Major conformation defects in the structure of the hoof include:

(1) Flared foot (figure 17): The sides of the hoof wall, particularly near the ground, are spread out. This is generally caused by neglect or poor trimming—forcing the horse's

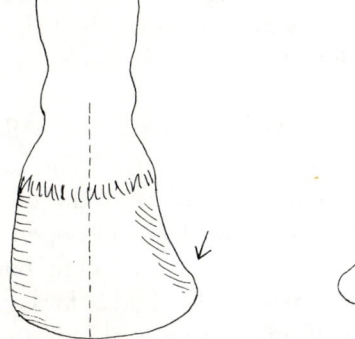

Figure 17. **Flared foot** (front view). 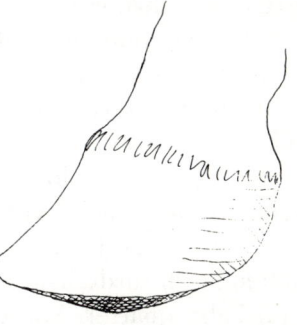　　Figure 18. Dropped sole.

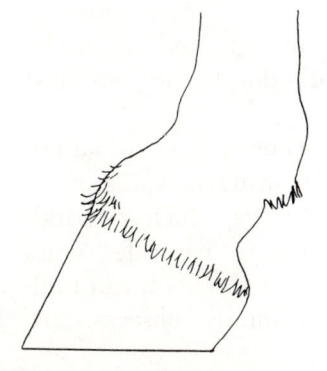

Figure 19. Buttress foot. 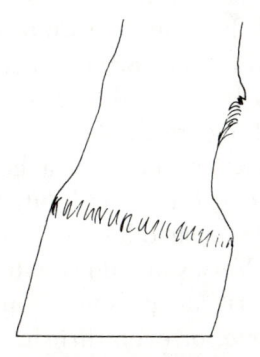　　Figure 20. Club foot.

weight unequally on the bearing wall. The flare marks a concussion point, which in turn stimulates abnormal hoof growth. This condition can be corrected by reshaping the foot gradually, usually removing no more than half the thickness of the wall per shoeing.

(2) Flat foot: In this condition, the hoof lacks its normal dome. The flat footed horse often walks on its heels to avoid sole pressure. Flat feet are almost always congenital, and mostly occur in the front feet. To remove the unwanted pressure from the sole (which is not designed to bear weight) the farrier should shoe the horse with a wide webbed shoe. Flat feet are not common in light horse breeds but occur sometimes in draft animals.

(3) Dropped sole (figure 18): This is a severe case of flat feet, and is often associated with chronic laminitis.* The sole may actually protrude below the bearing surface of the hoof wall. Generally the sole is very thick and flaky. Dropped sole is very serious, as it often indicates that the coffin bone has rotated downwards. The horse should be shod as for laminitis.

(4) False quarter: You will notice a vertical indentation in the hoof wall, parallel to the tubules. It will be flat, or even concave. This is not a true crack, but is due to a defect in the coronary band, caused by an injury such as tread. Since the inner quarter is the weaker of the two, it is most often affected. It occurs most often in the front feet. Nothing can be done until the coronary band heals (if it does). The hoof must simply be allowed to grow out.

(5) Rings in the hoof (fever rings): There are some natural irregularities in even a healthy hoof owing to variation in climate, exercise, and nutrition. These rings, which are parallel with each other and are fairly straight, are called grass rings. Very wavy lines, which widen near the heels can indicate past or present trouble with laminitis, abscess, low ringbone, or even thrush.

(6) Buttress foot (figure 19): This is a hard swelling near the coronary band in front and indicates a problem beneath, such

as low ringbone, an abscess, or possibly an old fracture of the coffin bone near its top (extensor process).

(7) Club foot (figure 20): This is a serious deformity where the axis is sixty degrees or more. Sometimes the hoof is even turned over. If it occurs in one foot only, the cause was probably an injury which prevented the animal from using the foot correctly for a long time and the tendons may have contracted. When the defect is bilateral (that is—occurs on both front feet), it was either congenital or possibly due to poor nutrition for the young foal. Often the superficial flexor tendon or even the suspensory ligament are contracted also.

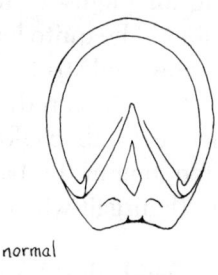

normal

Figure 21. Normal and contracted heels.

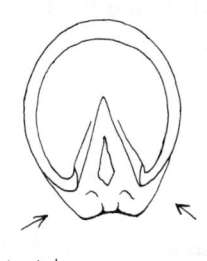

contracted

(8) Contracted heels (figure 21): In this condition the width of the horse's hoof at the heel is less than one quarter the circumference of the hoof at ground level. Besides indicating insufficient blood circulation in the foot, it may mean another problem is present. For a fuller discussion, see the lameness **section on page 99.**

64 CONFORMATION

Next observe the angle of the hoof and pastern. Ideally, in front feet, this should be about 50 degrees, and a little greater behind (figure 12). Hoof angle is important because it affects both the quality of the ride and the quality of the horse. A horse with stumpy, upright pasterns is going to have a rough trot, and his legs will be subjected to more concussion than is desirable. This is a factor conducive to ringbone and like problems. (This sort of conformation usually accompanies a straight shoulder.) See the model horse diagram.

The cannon bone should be fairly short, the knees broad and thick. The forearm should be well muscled and the chest broad, allowing for plenty of room for the heart and lungs. The shoulder should be quite long and sloping, as this permits a longer, more powerful stride. It also has more shock absorbing capacity and will thus reduce concussion.

Closely allied to limb conformation is the length of the back. Horses too long in the back sometimes develop an odd lateral swing in their gait which encourages speedy cutting or cross-firing.

On the other hand, the short-backed horse, when coupled with over-long legs, is prone to overreaching and forging. Forging occurs when the hind foot strikes the inner surface of the shoe or foot of the foreleg on the same side. It generally occurs at the trot.

FOOT FLIGHT

Ideally, the foot should break over right at the toe, and the foot should travel in a round arc. The heels should touch just before the toe, and the center of weight be located at the point of the frog.

When you are certain what traits to look for individually, it is time to consider the leg as a whole. To do this, you will need to view both front and hind limbs from two positions—anterior, or frontal, and lateral, or from the side.

THE IDEAL FORELEGS—ANTERIOR VIEW
(Figure 22b)

The horse's weight should be *evenly distributed* on both front legs. Any reluctance of the horse to bear weight on any leg, front or back, should be viewed with deepest suspicion, as it indicates not a conformation fault but an injury. The legs themselves should be quite straight; if you were to drop a plumb line from the point of the shoulder (tuberspinae) it should divide the entire leg lengthwise (radius, knee, cannon, and fetlock) into two equal sections. It should pass right behind the heels. Not many horses are in fact perfectly straight in front, but too large a deviation puts great strain on the collateral ligaments. The knees should "face front"—that is, not deviate toward or away from each other—and the cannon bone ought to be directly beneath the knee, not deviated to the outside.

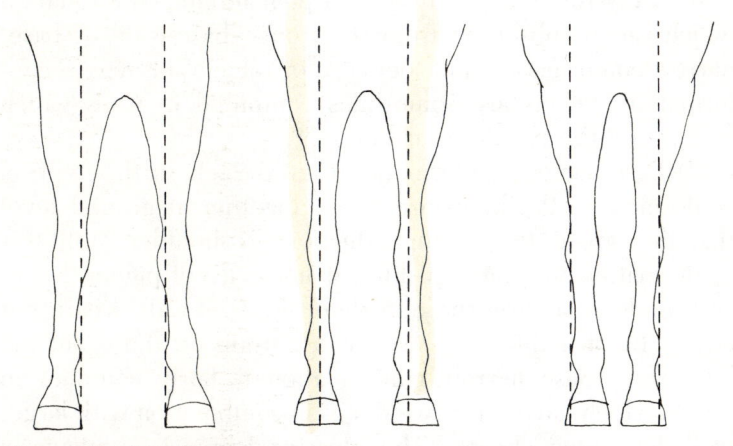

Figure 22. Foreleg: Anterior view.
a) Base-wide, b) Ideal, c) Base-narrow.

The toes should point straight ahead—that is the horse should be neither pigeon toed or splayfooted—and they should be as far apart at the ground as they were at their origin.

IDEAL FORELEGS—LATERAL VIEW (Figure 29b)

Straightness is again the quality you want, except in the shoulder and fetlock. The knee should not deviate either to the front or back, and it should not look as though a hunk of leg were removed either in front or behind it. The foot and pastern axis should have the same angle, ideally about 50 degrees.

CONFORMATION FAULTS OF THE FORELEG—ANTERIOR VIEW

Basically there are two types of poor foreleg conformation which can be observed from the front—base-wide or base-narrow conformation and toeing-in or toeing-out. These conformation defects are sometimes combined in ways which complicate the problem further.

(1) Base-narrow conformation (figure 22c): In this type of conformation, the hoofs are closer together at ground level than they are at their origin at the point of shoulder. With this conformation the horse paddles (particularly if pigeon toed), and tends to land on the outside of the hoof wall, wearing it down. In turn this causes a greater strain on those outside ligaments. Base narrow conformation is fairly common in horses which have short, wide legs in combination with large, well developed chests. (The Quarter Horse is particularly prone to this problem.)

Therapeutic trimming measures are called for, if they will not result in excessive strain. The farrier should lower the *inside* hoof wall, and use a light shoe. Neither heel calks nor a rolled toe shoe should be used on horses that paddle.

(2) Base-wide conformation (figure 22a): This condition is just the opposite of base-narrow conformation, but is more serious, particularly if accompanied by a toeing-out problem. The hoofs are wider apart at ground level than they are at their point of origin—the entire leg deviates to the outside. The horse will move with a wide-going gait. This condition is found most often in horses with poorly developed chests, such as the American Saddlebred or Tennessee Walking Horse. Some Thoroughbreds and Quarter Horses are also affected. Long-legged horses in general are predisposed. In several cases the horse may interfere; that is, one foot may strike or rub against the opposite foot or leg. This happens because the foot will break over towards the inside of the toe, and move in an inward arc known as "winging-in." Base wide horses take most strain on the inside of the hoof, and the indicated trimming procedure is to lower the outside wall to level the hoof.

(3) Toed-out conformation (figure 23c): This condition, also known as splayfooted, occurs when the pastern and hoof twist outward. It is usually congenital, but lack of proper trimming can aggravate the problem. Most of the horse's weight is placed on the inside of the hoof, wearing it down. (The outside half of the foot will sometimes be flared in compensation.) This can be found in horses with base-wide, base-narrow or even otherwise ideal conformation. In any case, a toed-out horse generally tends to wing to the inside. In bad cases, he may interfere. The treatment is to lower the outside of the hoof, in order to get the center of weight back onto the center of the hoof.

(4) Toed-in conformation (figure 23a): This common fault, also known as pigeon-toed, is congenital, but can be partially corrected if therapeutic shoeing is begun early enough. The hoof and pastern, in this case, are rotated inward and the horse tends to paddle; that is, break over the outside of the

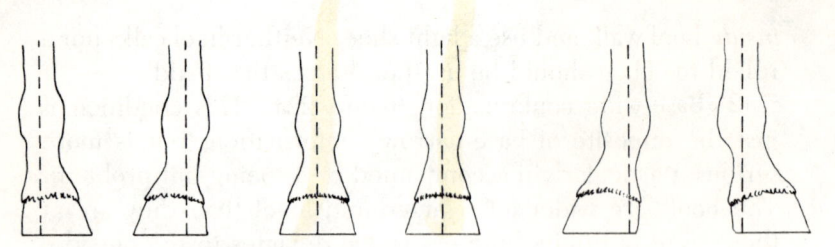

Figure 23. Foreleg: Anterior view.
a) Toed-in, b) Ideal, c) Toed-out.

toe and land on the inside. Consequently, more weight is placed on the outside of the foot. The inside of the hoof may be flared. The trimming indicated is to lower the inside of the hoof.

SOME FAULT COMBINATIONS

(1) Base-narrow, toed-in (figure 24b): In this case, there is great strain on the lateral collateral ligaments in both fetlock and pastern joints. As a result, the horse is prone to windpuffs, ringbone, and sidebone. This conformation also leads to paddling, and sometimes to interference at the fetlock joint. The farrier should trim the outside of the hoof to level it.

(2) Base-narrow, toed-out (figure 24a): This conformation is extremely weak. The horse tends to both wing and interfere, and there is a great strain placed on the ligaments below the fetlock. The horse may plait; that is, place one forefoot directly in front of the other. Horses which plait are prone to stumbling. The hoof tends to land to the outside; probably the inside of the hoof needs to be lowered. Observe carefully, however, to make sure if indeed the outside of the hoof is receiving the greater wear.

CONFORMATION

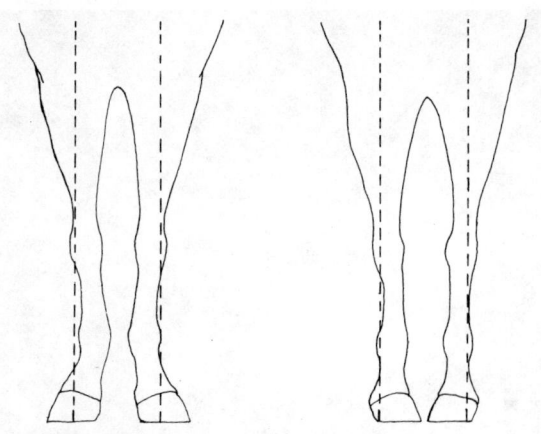

Figure 24. Foreleg: Anterior view.
a) Base-narrow/toed-out, b) Base-narrow/toed-in.

(3) Base-wide, toed-out (figure 25a): This combination puts the most stress on the inside of the leg. Generally the foot breaks over on the inside of the hoof. The outside needs to be lowered to level the hoof.

(4) Base-wide, toed-in (figure 25b): This is a rather unusual combination, where the horse breaks over on the inside of the toe. Again most of the strain is on the inside of the limb. Correct trimming depends on which side of the hoof receives the most wear; lower the other side.

(5) Bowlegged conformation (figure 26b): This condition, technically known as lateral deviation, is often accompanied by a base-narrow, toed-in conformation. It is usually congenital, but can be caused by nutritional deficiencies like rickets. Bowlegs place excessive strain on the carpal ligaments. Balancing the foot by proper trimming will relieve some of the strain, but the condition itself cannot be altered.

(6) Knock-kneed conformation (figure 26a): In this case the knees will deviate towards each other. Again, this is a congenital or nutritional problem, and the only treatment is to at-

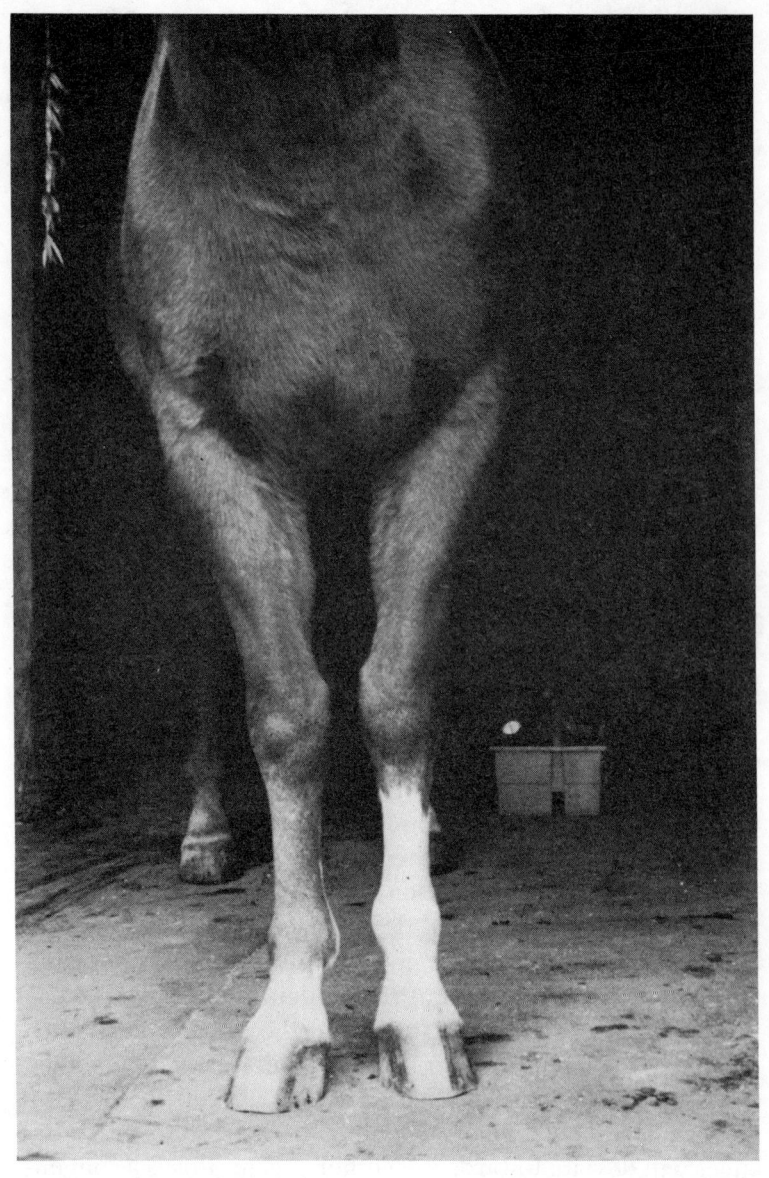

Base-narrow, toed-out. This horse also has a tendency to founder.

CONFORMATION 71

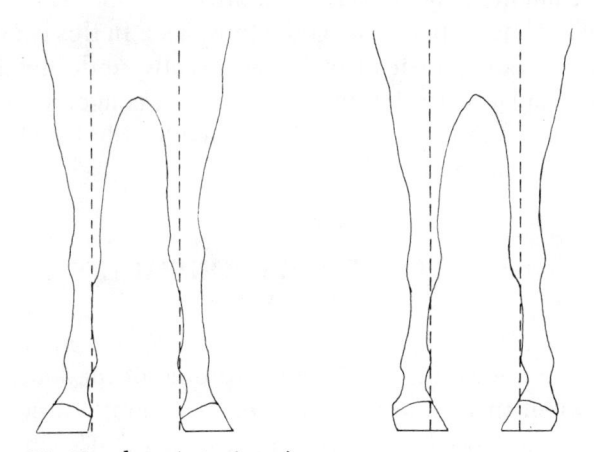

Figure 25. Foreleg: Anterior view.
a) Base-wide/toed-out, b) Based-wide/toed-in.

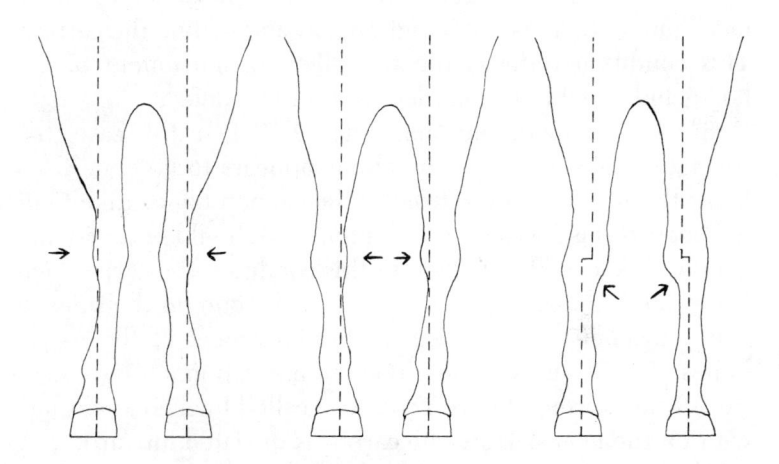

Figure 26. Foreleg: Anterior view.
a) Knock-kneed, b) Bow-legged, c) Off-set knees (bench-legged).

tempt to balance the foot to relieve the strain on the inferior check ligaments and the stay apparatus.

(7) Offset knees (bench-legged, figure 26c): In this condition the cannon bone, instead of being directly underneath the knee, is displaced to the outside. This is a congenital condition, which often predisposes the animal to splints. The hoof should be balanced to relieve strain.

FORELEG CONFORMATION FAULTS—
LATERAL VIEW

(1) Open knees (figure 27b): The profile of the knee looks lumpy when this condition is present. Generally it occurs at the lower end of the radius "growth plate." Usually open knees are caused by a mineral imbalance in the young, growing horse, and becomes less noticeable as the horse grows older.

(2) Tied-in knees (figure 27a): A large piece seems to be taken out of the horse's leg right below and behind the carpus. This condition reduces the free, flowing movement of the horse and should be regarded as a serious defect.

(3) Cut-out under the knees (figure 27c): In this case, the reverse of tied-in knees, the chunk appears to be gone from beneath the knee on the front of the cannon bone. Like tied-in knees, this is a weak conformation, and should be avoided.

(4) Calf knees (figure 28a): In this condition the carpal joint is deviated towards the back. This puts strain on the inferior check ligament and the entire frontal aspect of the carpal bones. This is an extremely poor conformation.

(5) Knee-sprung (figure 28b): Also called bucked knees and over on the knees. Here the carpus is deviated forward. This condition is often present at birth, but may disappear in a few months. It is, at any rate, not so severe as calf knees, but it does put strain on the suspensory ligament, the superficial

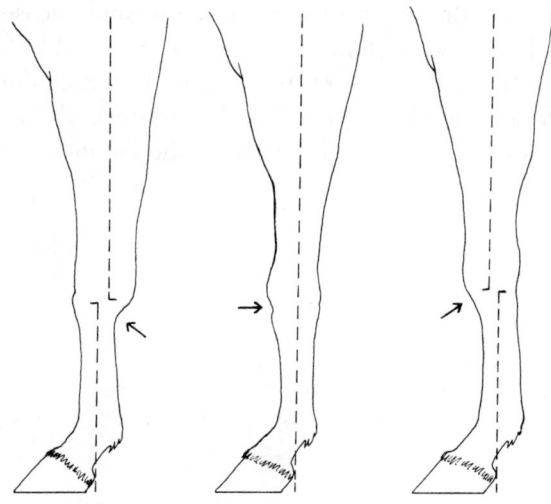

Figure 27. Foreleg: Lateral view.
a) Tied-in knees, b) Open knees, c) Cut-out under the knees.

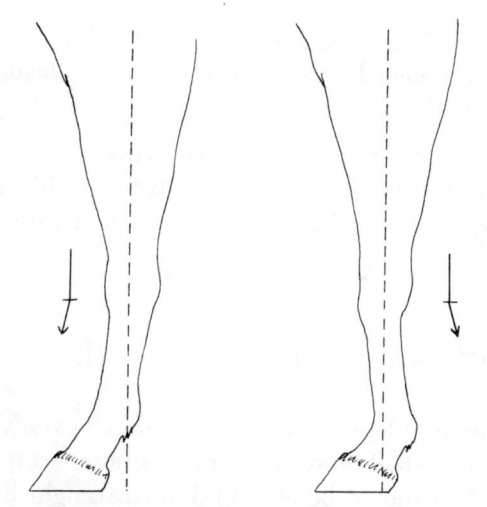

Figure 28. Foreleg: Lateral view.
a) Calf-knees, b) Knee-sprung (bucked knees).

flexor tendon, the extensor carpi radialis, and the sesamoid bones. A knee-sprung horse is quite apt to stumble.

(6) Standing under in front (figure 29c): In this conformation the whole front leg looks too far backward beneath the horse's body. This causes too much strain on the ligaments and tendons.

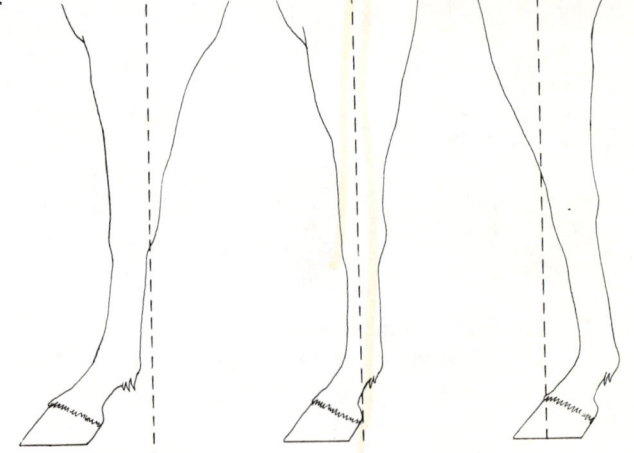

Figure 29. Foreleg: Lateral view.
    a) Camped-in in front, b) Ideal, c) Standing-under in front.

(7) Camped in front (figure 29a): This stance is generally adopted by the horse when he is experiencing pain in the front limbs. It should therefore be regarded with deep suspicion.

THE IDEAL HINDLEG—POSTERIOR VIEW

As in the front legs, the weight should be evenly distributed on each foot, so that there is no undue strain on any structure of the limb. You should be able to draw a straight line from the center of the hindquarters through the hock, cannon bone, fetlock, and hoof. The hocks should be fairly large and smooth.

THE IDEAL HINDLEGS—LATERAL VIEW (Figure 31b)

A straight line drawn from the tuber ischii should pass along the rear of the metatarus. In other words, the back of the cannon bone should be directly underneath the point of the rump. The stifle should not be too straight, and the hock angle neither too straight nor too angular. The horse shown is just right.

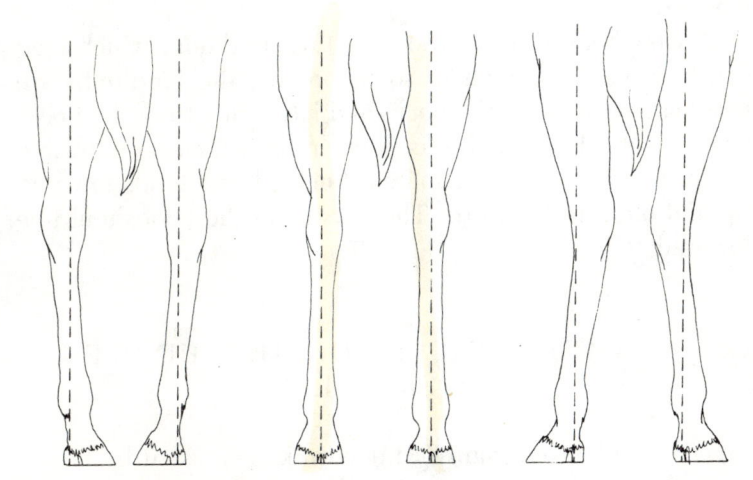

Figure 30. Hindleg: Posterior view.
a) Base-narrow, accompanied by bow-legged, b) Ideal, c) Cow-hocked.

CONFORMATION FAULTS OF THE HINDLEGS—POSTERIOR VIEW

As in the forelegs, horses can be afflicted with a base-wide or base-narrow conformation. Refer back to that section for complete information.

(1) Base-narrow and bowlegged conformation (figure 30a): This is a rather common combination; the hocks will deviate away from each other. This is a congenital condition, and usually indicates weak hocks. The inside hoof wall should be lowered.

(2) Cow-hocked (figure 30c): In this condition, which incidently is very common in some breeds, the hindlimbs are base-narrow as far as the hocks and base-wide from the hocks to the hoofs. Thus the hocks point in toward each other, and cause the toes to be splayfooted. Such a horse tends to wing-in, and often to interfere. The outside of the hoof should be lowered.

CONFORMATION FAULTS OF THE HINDLEGS—LATERAL VIEW

(1) Sickle-hocked (figure 31a): Also known as curby hocks. Here there is an angulation of the hock joints. In other words, there is a forward deviation of the hindleg below the hock so that the horse looks as if he were standing too far under. This is a congenital problem and one which can easily lead to bone spavin and curb.

(2) Straight behind or post-legged (figure 31c): This is the opposite condition from sickle hocks. There is too little angulation in the hock and stifle joints; the pasterns also may be straight. Sometimes, however, the pastern and hoof may have a broken back axis in an attempt to compensate for the lack of

CONFORMATION 77

Cow hocks. This pony was retrieved after a chase (through the mud, obviously) to display a fine example of cow hocks.

spring. Although less serious than sickle hocks, this sort of leg is easily strained, and predisposes the horse to bog spavin and upward fixation of the patella.

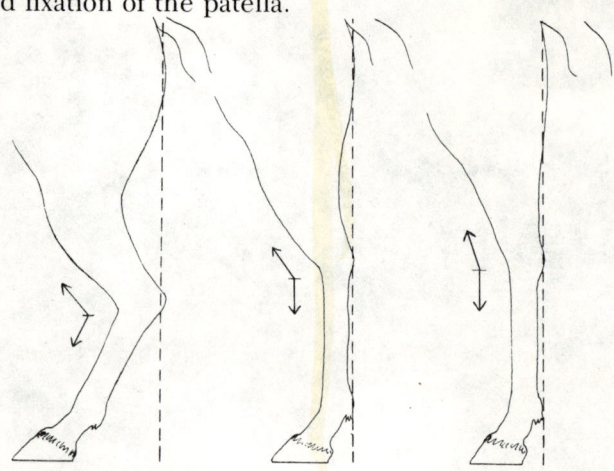

Figure 31. Hindleg: Lateral view.
    a) Sickle-hocked, b) Ideal, c) Straight-behind (post-legged).

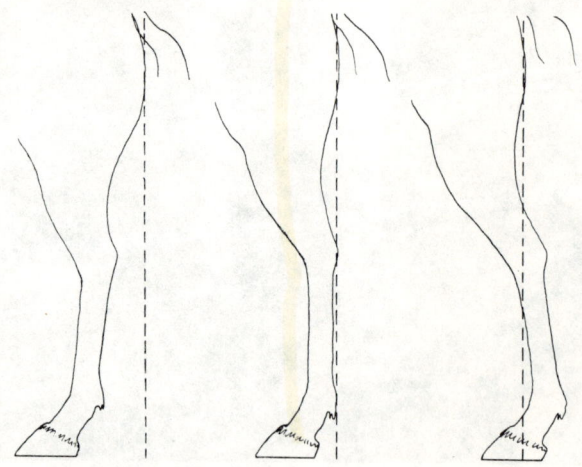

Figure 32. Hindleg: Lateral view.
    a) Standing-under behind, b) Ideal, c) Camped behind.

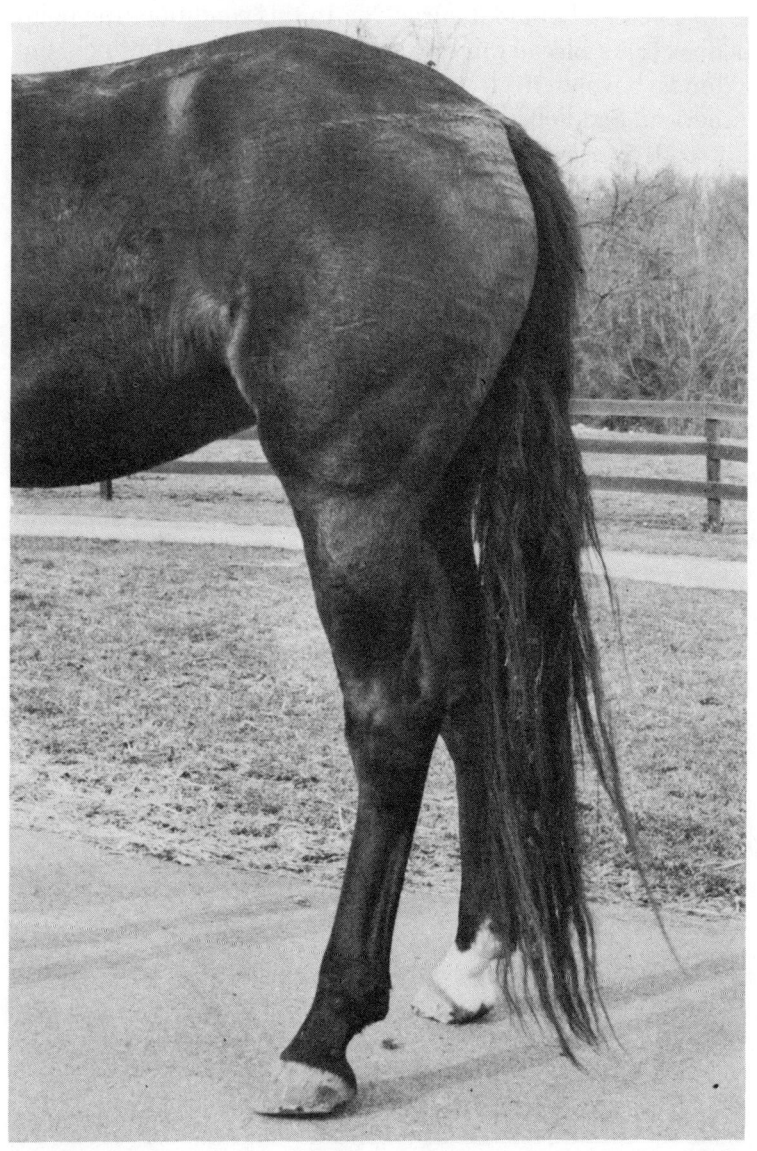

Straight behind. The too-straight hind legs of this otherwise lovely filly resulted in upward fixation of the patella.

(3) Camped behind (figure 32c): In this condition, the point of hock is not placed directly beneath the point of buttock, but extends beyond it. It is also the "parked position" of the American Saddlebred, Tennessee Walker, and Morgan show horse. It is acceptable in the show ring, but when it occurs naturally it is a conformation defect.

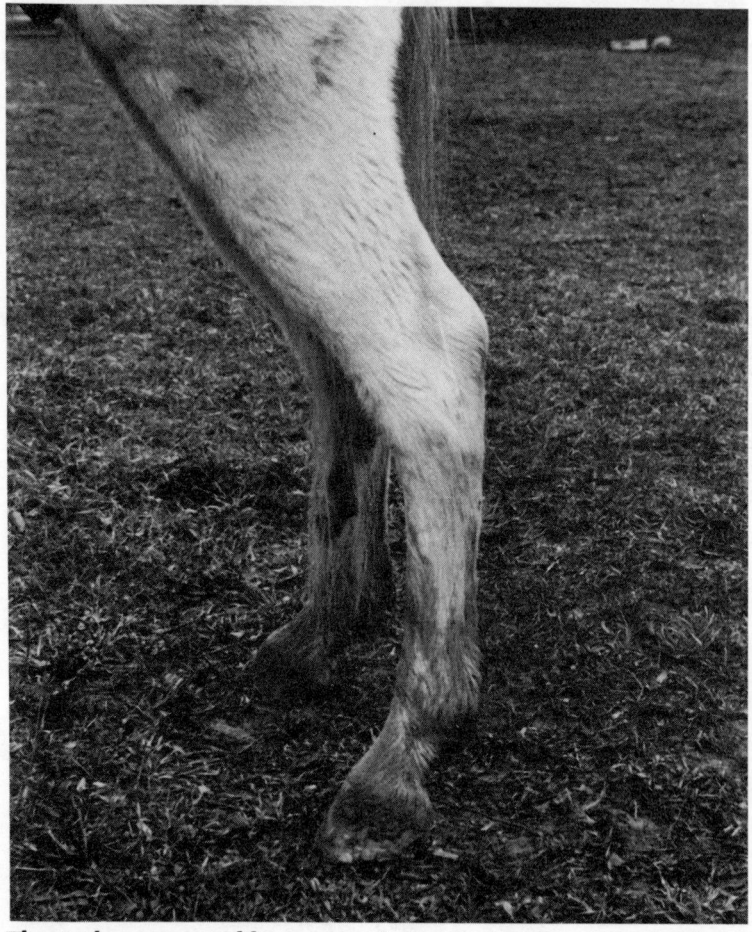

This is the same muddy pony as shown previously. Note that he is camped behind as well as cow hocked.

CHAPTER 8

Lameness

PREFATORY REMARKS

The last part of this handbook is divided into three sections: lameness examination, descriptions of horse lamenesses, and simplified diagnosis charts. These sections supplement one another and should be used together. For instance, in the examination section, an asterisk (*) after a word refers you to the lamenesses section to seek additional information under that heading, and while Diagnosis Chart A lists common symptoms of different lameness types, the best method for observing or eliciting those symptoms is found in the examination section. If you think you have located the *area* of the ailment, but have not identified the problem more specifically, see Diagnosis Chart B. This chart lists the common problems affecting each area of the horse's foot and leg.

Lameness is not an isolated phenomenon. It does not simply occur: it always has a cause. In other words, horses do not just "go lame." It is up to the horse owner to discover the cause when he considers lameness. Lameness is not a disease or ailment in itself, but an indication of a disorder somewhere in the body. And it does not help matters much to know that the cause of the lameness may be far indeed from where the lameness manifests itself. Lameness can be described functionally as something which interferes with the animal's normal mode of progression. It is often, but not always, accompanied by pain. (Mechanical lameness, caused by joint stiffness, for instance, is not painful). Lameness may be caused by:

(1) Poor conformation, which can predispose the horse to various ailments;

(2) Trauma such as a direct blow, puncture wounds, falls, tendon or ligament strain or sprain, burns, wrenches, etc.;

(3) Lack of proper attention to the feet, including unhygienic conditions and poor shoeing practices;

(4) Nutritional or metabolic problems;

(5) Excess weight (particularly in combination with small hoof size);

(6) Anomaly in the spine, or other parts of the nervous system or inner ear (these systems affect a horse's coordination);

(7) Fatigue;

or any combination of these!

Lamenesses are often divided into two types: supporting leg and swinging leg lameness. Supporting leg lameness manifests itself when the horse places his weight on the affected limb. Most commonly, this indicates that the lameness site is below the knee, and the bones, joints, hoof, and collateral ligaments are suspect.

Swinging leg lameness is more obvious as the horse moves, particularly when he attempts to raise the affected leg. It generally occurs above the knee and the most commonly injured structures are joint capsules, muscles, and tendons.

For certain lamenesses, the dysfunction may occur at both phases of the stride—lifting and supporting.

Another factor to be considered is the "complementary lameness" phenomenon. What this means is that a horse, experiencing pain in one forelimb, may shift more weight to the other forelimb to relieve the strain. The unaccustomed weight will put a strain on the suspensory ligaments, flexor tendons, and sesamoid bones of a previously sound leg, and cause that one too, eventually to be lame. It should be noted that a horse lame in both front feet may exhibit fewer outward signs of lameness than when only one foot is affected. Complementary lameness can also occur when the horse, because of discomfort, shifts his weight from one part of his leg to another; for example, from the heel to the toe, with the same result.

There is an old Cockney saying: "Hit hain't the 'eavy 'aulin' wot 'urts the 'orse's 'ooves; it's the 'ammer, 'ammer, 'ammer on the 'ot, 'ard 'ighway." This is another, and more picturesque, way of saying that concussion is bad for your horse. Concussion, which is increased by certain conformation faults, such as upright pasterns, jars muscles and tendons and can inflame bone surfaces. When an inflammation sets in, blood rushes to the site, resulting eventually in the deposit of calcium. This sets up new bony growth—which, in essence, is what ringbone, splints, and bone spavin amount to. Especially is this true of young horses.

So please, be kind to your horse and use common sense about where, how long, and how hard you ride him.

Although it is important to keep in mind that there is no substitute for a veterinarian's experience and training, you can learn to make an intelligent examination of your horse. But before you can go about confidently examining your horse for lameness, you must know what he looks like, feels like, and acts like when he is sound. This is where your knowledge can be invaluable both to yourself and your veterinarian in case Claude, your hypothetical horse, does become lame. Only you will be able to tell if a particular bump is hours, weeks, or months old. Only you know if the horse "always acts like that" when he trots. Being able to differentiate between the normal, although perhaps idiosyncratic, behavior of your horse and a lameness may spell the difference between a correct and an incorrect diagnosis. So as you read through this section on examination techniques for discovering lameness, try them out on Claude now while (hopefully) he's still healthy.

LAMENESS EXAMINATION

So what do you do when one day your horse comes down lame? Call the vet? Have a drink? Wrap the leg and hope it gets better? Shoot poor old Claude? No. The *first* thing you should do is to look at each hoof and see if there isn't a nail sticking out of the bottom of it. If there is, pull it out and then call the veterinarian so he can give Claude a tetanus shot. You will find that about 90 percent of lamenesses occur in the foot, and a large fraction of these are puncture wounds. It never hurts to do the obvious thing first. Even if you don't see a nail, however, don't rule out a puncture; they are insidious things that show up days later, long after the exciting cause has vanished—all too often right into the foot.

At any rate, if you are satisfied that there is no nail easily visible, the next thing you must do is to make a systematic examination of the entire animal. Here's how (most lamenesses in riding horses occur in the forelegs so we should begin there):

Examination for Foreleg Lameness

First you need to ascertain which leg is in fact the lame one. For this you should bring your horse outside, so that you can observe his gaits. Have him handled by a person he knows well, and keep the lead line fairly loose. At the walk, a horse will generally lift his head when the lame foot, especially if it is a forefoot, strikes the ground. Any lameness that you observe at this gait will worsen at the trot, where you must listen as well as look. Instead of an even two-beat rhythm, the lame hoof, whether fore or hind, will strike the ground more lightly than the sound one. If both front feet are lame, the horse will travel in a stiff, pottery way. Normally a horse lands heel first.

If the horse goes on his toe, it could indicate a problem in the heel region of the foot.

To determine if the lameness is swinging leg lameness or supporting leg lameness (the second type is more common), make the horse step over an obstacle. A horse with swinging leg lameness will either refuse to do so at all, or else comply only with reluctance and obvious pain. The horse with supporting leg lameness will have no trouble lifting his leg over the obstacle, although he may evidence pain as the foot is set down again.

To check for hind leg lameness (rarer than lameness in the foreleg), watch the hindquarters as the horse is trotted away from you. If a hindleg lameness exists, the sound quarter will be more active than the other; that is, it will rise and drop farther.

Turn the animal in a circle (a horse with hock problems may refuse to move in a tight circle at all). Supporting leg lameness generally worsens when that leg is to the inside of the circle (there is more weight on that foot), while those animals with swinging leg lameness do worse when the affected leg is to the outside.

In addition, if possible, test the horse on both hard and soft ground, uphill and downhill. Notice also if the lameness increases or decreases with exercise. Take careful note of all you have discovered, so that if you need your veterinarian you will be able to give him an accurate account of what you have observed.

Now that you have ascertained the lame leg, proceed with the examination to discover the location more specifically.

First of all, carry out your examination in a place your horse knows well, such as his stable. It's best if no strangers are present, for the less Claude has to distract him, the better. As you note symptoms, *jot them down* for reference to the diagnosis chart.

Always begin the examination with the foot. Even if you notice swellings higher in the leg, the chances are still good that the seat of the trouble is in the hoof. Try to line up the forelegs evenly with each other, and compare them.

If the horse continually "points," you may not be able to do this. Pointing is evidence of considerable amounts of pain. Normally horses rest a hind foot only when they stand, keeping both forefeet on the ground. If lameness is present in both front feet, the horse may point first one, then the other.

Feel for heat in each hoof with the back of your hand. If uncertain about this, sometimes wetting both hoofs with a sponge helps. (If one hoof is in fact hotter than the other, the water will evaporate more quickly from it.) Notice if one forefoot seems different in size from the other—higher, narrower, or flatter. Then tap the wall, quarters, and heel lightly with a hammer, listening for a hollow sound. This could indicate an abscess.

Check also for dryness and cracks, as sometimes a crack can pinch the sensitive laminae inside. If you know how, remove the shoes and scrub the hoof clean. Examine each nail as it comes from the hoof to make sure there is no blood on it which would indicate a nail prick. This is especially important if the lameness manifests itself within a few days after shoeing. Check for any black spots or lines at the "white line" which may mean migration of foreign material into the hoof. Red spots are often symptoms of recent bruises; yellow spots are older ones. Blue spots can be warnings of developing abscesses.

Examine the frog to see if it is of good quality and maintaining contact with the ground. Thrush is evidenced by a foul odor and deteriorating condition of the frog. Check the heels for contraction; remember, the horse's heels should be about one-quarter of the circumference of the hoof.

If you have hoof testers, use them to find any sensitive areas. If the whole sole seems painful, laminitis, fracture, or a large infection from a puncture wound may be present. If the sensitive area is under the frog, and there is no puncture, there is a possibility of navicular disease.*

LAMENESS

Moving up the leg, feel the coronary band for heat or swelling. Palpate it from side to side with the tips of your fingers and notice if there is any bony enlargement beneath or a roughening of the hair near the front. This may indicate a low ringbone. If there is drainage from the coronary area, a puncture wound or migration of foreign material from within the hoof is the probable cause.

Next examine the lateral cartilages for flexibility. Do this first when the foot is on the ground, then flex the knee and hold the hoof backward; see if any calcification has occurred; if so, sidebone is probably present, but as sidebone is seldom a cause of lameness in itself, do not abandon your search.

Press deeply into each heel with your finger and check for pain, sensitivity, or exudate. Serious cases of thrush can invade the area between the bulbs of the heel.

Working your way up the horse's pastern, feel the pulsation of the digital arteries by placing one thumb on the inner aspect. Normal pulse for a horse is 35 to 40 beats per minute. A full, throbbing pulse indicates congestion within the foot, and is symptomatic of laminitis and other diseases. Hoof testers should confirm this diagnosis. Be sure to compare both legs. High temperatures and swellings in the pastern area also may point to ringbone; feel for the characteristic enlargements. Unfortunately, the really painful phase of ringbone occurs before the enlargements are present, or at least noticeable. Only X-rays can confirm the suspicion that ringbone is present.

Examination of the fetlock joint is next on the agenda. Look for swellings, but remember that foot lameness is often responsible for *painless* swellings in the fetlock. If there is pain on pressure over the sesamoid bones, suspect sesamoiditis and related ills. If the swelling is to the front of the joint, osselets or a chip fracture of the long pastern are likely culprits.

The cannon bone itself is a *relatively* sturdy structure and unlikely to be at fault, but the front of it should be checked for bucked shins, which are characterized by a vague but painful swelling. This is primarily a condition of young race horses in heavy training (and if your horse has it, shame on you).

Just behind the cannon bone lies the suspensory ligament. The damage it is subject to generally occurs near the lower third of the cannon bone, where the ligament begins to branch. Pain when you press here may indicate damage to this important structure.

Feel the splint bones from where they are connected to the cannon bone by ligaments to their nodules further down the leg. Splints* are common in horses under four years of age.

About the middle of the cannon bone lies the inferior check ligament, which attaches the deep flexor tendon to the cannon bone. Damage to it is indicated by pain on pressure.

The flexor tendons, both of them, should be examined both with weight on the leg and with the leg flexed. If there is swelling it will probably occur just above the fetlock joint (see bowed tendon* and tenosynovitis).

Next examine the knee. Look for swellings both in front and back. A swelling in the back towards the inside may indicate a fracture of the accessory carpal bones. Swellings on the front are likely to be swollen joint capsules. If the swelling is very hard, carpitis or a fracture should be considered. Flex the knee to see if pain is caused by this movement. When flexing the knee, remember that with a normal horse the heel can be made to touch or almost touch the elbow.

The forearm should be checked for swellings and pain (most likely caused by puncture wounds).

Check the elbow next. If it has a "dropped" appearance, and the horse is unable to put weight on that foot, consider radial paralysis.*

If the muscles of the shoulder and forearm seem small or weak, it may be a sign that muscle atrophy has taken place as a result of a long standing problem (*not* necessarily in the shoulder or forearm). Check the bursa at the point of shoulder; if it seems painful or swollen, consider bicipital bursitis.*

Examination for Hindleg Lameness

In most respects, examination for hindleg lameness resembles examination for frontleg lameness, but there are some additional things to check for.

The hock joint is a common site for hindleg lameness. It is subject to curb,* thoroughpin,* capped hock,* bog spavin,* bone spavin,* and occult spavin.* There is an excellent test for bone spavin which ought always to be included when there is any suspicion of rear leg lameness. Reasonably enough, it is called the spavin test, and requires the horse to trot, so it should be conducted outside. Lift the rear leg and flex it as much as you can, and hold it that way for two minutes, as nearly as you can manage. Then trot the horse immediately afterward. If the lameness is much increased at this point, suspect bone spavin or occult spavin. A swelling to the rear of the hock indicates curb while other swellings in the region may be bog spavin or, a little higher up, thoroughpin.

The stifle joint should be checked next. It is subject to a condition technically known as "upward fixation of the patella"* but more commonly known, in stable parlance, as being "stifled." This means that the knee cap, or patella, has slipped upward and locked, so that the horse can no longer flex the joint. It is unmistakable when it occurs, but often, especially in young horses, it is an intermittent occurance. Grasp the patella and feel for the firmness of its attachment. Feel also for any unusual swellings in the area which could indicate incipient gonitis.*

LAMENESSES

Arthritis

Definition and Causes: Arthritis, or, as it used to be called, rheumatism, is an inflammation of a joint. As in humans, it can strike anywhere in the body and can attack bones, ligaments, or joint capsules. Its favorite sites are pastern, fetlock, knee, shoulder, and elbow in the forelegs, and hock, stifle, and hip in the rear—the focal points of concussion.

Concussion is in fact a major cause of arthritis, particularly in older animals with weak conformation. Sometimes, a direct blow or other wrenching trauma is the original source of the problem. Even influenza and other diseases have been blamed. From whatever primary cause, however, arthritis when it first strikes may not cause any irreversible damage, especially when it originates from a trauma such as a kick or fall. When arthritis first occurs, the synovial fluid increases in response to the inflammation. This condition is called serous arthritis and it swells the membrane which surrounds the joint. In this case the inflammation is usually fairly mild. As long as the horse is rested, and the joint is not subjected to any further stress, the arthritis, while it will not go away, will not worsen or cause lameness (though the horse may be a little stiff).

If, however, the stress is continued, or if the arthritic area becomes infected, the outlook is much poorer. Continued stress on the joint may result in what is called osteoarthritis. Osteoarthritis can even result from a too enthusiastic use of corticoids (which inhibit the natural healing powers of the body) to treat serous arthritis. In this condition, the cartilage and the bone themselves are affected, not just the joint. At this stage the damage is permanent.

Worst of all is infectious arthritis, in which the original serous arthritis has become complicated by some sort of infection, usually borne by the bloodstream. Foals are sometimes born with a particular form of infectious arthritis known as "navel ill," which is often widespread throughout the body. (It is prevented by soaking the umbilical cord in iodine.) Infectious arthritis is an extremely potent disabler and can destroy joint cartilage in hours by the action of the enzymes of the foreign organisms which have been introduced. Recovery is rare, as treatment is seldom begun in time.

Symptoms: In an acute case (that is, one which has come on suddenly, as opposed to a chronic one, which occurs over a period of time), the horse may exhibit pain, sweating, heaving sides, blowing. Sometimes, however, these symptoms are absent. He may also have a temperature. The joint involved will be very hot and swollen with fluid, and will be painful to the touch. Generally the horse will be extremely reluctant to move and he will be quite lame.

Treatment: If the arthritis has not become infectious, absolute rest for at least four weeks is the best cure. The veterinarian may wish to use a local anesthetic to relieve pain and keep the horse calm. He may inject a corticoid to reduce inflammation, but this does not mean that the horse is ready to go back to work. Your veterinarian will give further advice about wraps, linaments, or hot packs to be used later.

If the arthritis has become infectious, antibiotics are needed, and quickly. Permanant lameness, however, nearly always results from cases of infectious arthritis.

Osteoarthritis can result from either of the other two kinds, and is known as a chronic arthritis. Bone damage has already occurred in this type. Old methods of treatment included firing and blistering, but as usual the claims for this type of therapy are mostly overrated. If the arthritis occurs in the hindlimbs, and the ends of the joint grow together (or ankylose), the horse may be able to return to work without pain.

Azoturia (Monday Morning Disease)

Definition and Causes: Azoturia is massive destruction of muscle cells which occurs in horses which are kept on high grain ration even when they are not being used. The azoturia strikes when the animal is returned to work after a period of rest (hence the nickname). The destruction is caused by the formation of lactic acid, which cannot be converted into glycogen quickly enough by the horse's body. This results in renal damage, which can cause death.

Symptoms: These appear almost immediately after the horse is returned to work. There will be tremors, incoordination, and heavy sweating. The urine will vary in color from light brown to black (due to the presence of myoglobin released during muscle destruction). This sympton gave this disease its old name "black water."

Treatment: Stop the horse immediately. Do not even try to move him back to the barn. If the horse does not go down, he may recover with rest and light diet.

Bicipital Bursitis

Definition and Causes: Not a true shoulder lameness, bicipital bursitis is an inflammation of the bicipital bursa in the front of the shoulder joint. This bursa encloses the biceps brachii muscles. The condition is usually caused by a blow at the point of shoulder or a severe slip which tears the tissue.

Symptoms: The horse will show both swinging and supporting leg lameness. He may refuse to move forward at all, but will back readily. Pulling the leg upward and backward will elicit pain. Other signs are the general symptoms for shoulder lameness.

Treatment: Although corticoids may be helpful, in general the horse will either recover in three months or never.

Bog Spavin

Definition and Causes: Technically known as tarsal hydrathrosis, bog spavin occurs when the synovial membrane of the tibiotarsal joint is distended. It is a common disorder which particularly affects upright joints. Bog spavin results from overwork, strain, concussion, or direct trauma. It occurs fairly often in Hackney ponies, Tennessee Walking Horses, or in any straight-hocked conformation. Vitamin and mineral imbalances have also been named as possible causes.

Symptoms: The bog spavin is a round, well-defined swelling which fluctuates on pressure. It may occur on the inner front or rear aspect of the tarsal joint. In recent cases the lesion may be hot and painful, and there may be lameness. Later the bog spavin will be cold and painless.

Treatment: In the acute stage, cold applications, astringents, and bandages should be used. (There are now bandages on the market which can effectively deal with this awkward part of the horse's anatomy.)

Bowed Tendon

Definition and Causes: Also known as tendosynovitis, tendovaginitis, or tendonitis, it is the partial rupture of the deep or superficial flexor tendon and its sheath. It is a common, and very serious, condition, and is the result of a severe strain to one or both tendons, usually the superficial flexor. The forelegs are commonly affected. Sometimes the connective fibers which make up the tendon are torn—generally in the middle third of the tendon. In this case, hemorrhage within the tendon can occur. When there is only a "bow" present, there is no discontinuity in the structure, although an excessive amount of blood, serum, and synovial fluid may be present in the area. Later scar tissue will develop between the tendon sheath and surrounding tissue.

Bowed tendons can result from any excessive strain to the flexor tendon: jumping, excessive speed, slipping, poor shoeing or trimming (long toe, low heel), or muscular fatigue (which is transmitted to the inelastic tendons). Horses with very long, sloping pasterns seem predisposed.

Symptoms: There will be heat over the tendons, and some soreness. Careful palpation of the tendons will reveal a thickening (but to be confident about this you should be familiar with how your horse feels ordinarily). Palpate the tendons both with the leg flexed, the cannon bone parallel to the ground, and with weight on it. There will be pain on pressure over the tendon, and, some hours later, diffuse swelling will occur. Although at first the horse may be only slightly lame, severe lameness may appear later. When this happens, the horse will stand with his heel raised to relieve the strain, and when he walks or trots will not permit the fetlock to drop. There is also the characteristic "bowed" appearance of the tendon. If the suspensory ligament and/or the check ligament are also involved, the situation is more serious. This is equally true if the tendon sheaths and ligament attachments have completely ruptured. In this case the fetlock will be dropped to the ground, as there is no longer anything to support it.

Treatment: A bowed tendon will never be as good as new, since the fibrous tissue does not have the elasticity of the normal tendon. Complete rest is mandatory for a period of a month to a year, depending on the severity of the bow. When it first occurs, cold water hosing and bandaging with an astringent should be tried. The veterinarian may inject a corticoid and try a plaster cast, from knee to hoof.

LAMENESS

When the horse is shod, the toe should be kept short and the heel raised. A special shoe with a raised heel may be used for a short period.

Bowed tendon is nearly always preventable. Sensible riding and training techniques should guard against the overwork of a tired animal.

Bruising

Definition and Causes: Bruises occur in horses just as they do in people. The most common location for bruises, the sole, is susceptible because it is not designed to bear weight, and is not very resilient. When a horse, especially a flat-footed horse, is fitted with shoes which allow pressure on the sole rather than on the weight-bearing structures (the wall and bars), he is liable to bruising. The damage can be serious since the bruise is not really in the horn of the foot but in the sensitive sole beneath it. In a really severe case, the damage can extend even to the coffin bone (see pedal osteitis*). If this is the case, many months may go by before the injury heals.

Symptoms: You will notice a discoloration in the sole of the hoof. New bruises are usually red in color and seem to be composed of little red speckles. If the bruise is an old one, the discoloration may be yellow or coppery. If the discoloration is bluish, it may indicate a developing abscess, which should be treated as a puncture wound. In addition, the horse may be lame, especially when travelling over hard and gravelly ground.

Treatment: Soaking the animal's foot may relieve the pain. If the shoes are the offending agent, remove them and have the horse shod with a wide-webbed shoe which puts no pressure on the sole. If the hoof conformation itself is at fault, it is sometimes effective to shorten the toe and trim the heel only slightly. The sole may in this instance thicken and form a better dome.

If the bruise has turned into an abscess, the sole must be trimmed away from the area to expose the sensitive structures underneath. A tetanus antitoxin should be administered and the foot treated with tincture of iodine as in a puncture wound.

Bucked Shins

Definition and Causes: This condition, also known as chin buck (an obvious mishearing), is a metacarpal periostitis, or inflammation of the periosteum of the cannon bone. It almost always occurs on both front legs at once. It is common in young Thoroughbreds in the early stages of heavy training and is caused by concussion, overexertion, or injury. When this occurs, the periosteum may loosen and hemorrhage occurs between it and the bone.

Symptoms: There is a warm swelling on the front of the cannon bone which is painful if pressed. It will eventually harden and thicken.

Treatment: Rest. Rest. Rest. The horse may recover completely if this therapy is used.

Bursitis

Definition and Causes: Bursitis, as its name indicates, refers to an inflammation of a bursa. A bursa, remember, allows different structures of the horse's body to slide over one another, by reducing the friction.

Bursitis can occur not only where there are actually bursae originally present; sometimes repeated concussion to an area results in a "false bursa." Capped elbow* is an example of this type of bursitis. Another common type of false, or acquired, bursitis is hygroma, which occurs on the front of the knee, and arises most often from trauma.

The worst aspect of bursitis is that the bursae often calcify, which can result in torn ligaments and tendons.

Symptoms: A swelling of the affected region, which may be either soft or hard, depending on whether its contents are primarily fluid or fibrous. Lameness, when present, is generally quite mild.

Treatment: Depending upon the stage of the bursitis, corticoids and surgical removal have been effective.

Canker

Definition and Causes: Canker is a nasty inflammation affecting the frog of the hoof, somewhat like thrush. Generally, however, canker is much worse, as it attacks the horn-secreting tissues of the hoof, and can spread to other parts of the hoof and sole. Though there is disagreement over the cause of canker, poor hygiene seems to be a factor. Canker most often occurs in draft horses with flattish feet. Fortunately, it is not as common today as it used to be.

Symptoms: Lameness may be present in the early stages; the frog will be quite loose and may even tear. Beneath the frog is the typical "thrushy" odor, and there will be an exudate, which, however, will be white rather than blackish. The tissue bleeds quite easily.

Treatment: Other than keeping the hoof clean and dry, there is little treatment that is effective against canker.

Capped Elbow or Shoe Boil

Definition and Causes: This is a bursitis of the olecranon process (point of elbow). It is a false bursa caused by irritation to the elbow. It occurs most often in gaited show horses, or those horses confined to a stall. Shoes most commonly are the source of the inflammation, as they press against the elbow.

Symptoms: There will be a tender swelling at the point of elbow which may vary greatly in size and hardness. It may or may not be inflamed.

Treatment: If caught early, cold water, astringents, and massage should be used. In addition, the cause of the irritation must be removed. If the swelling has abscessed, antibiotics are needed.

Capped Hock

Definition and Causes: Capped hock, like capped elbow,* is a bursitis (in this case of the calcanean process, rather than of the olecranon process). It is caused by an injury to the point of hock. Since there is normally no bursa at this site, capped hock is an acquired, or false, bursitis. If the tendon is involved, the swelling will be hard, and the condition is more serious.

Symptoms: Capped hock is generally classed as a blemish and rarely causes lameness. It may, however, be accompanied by curb. The swelling may be soft or hard, depending on whether or not the tendon is involved. New cases are hot and painful.

Treatment: Cold water should be applied in new cases, and corticoids can be injected, and a pressure bandage used. However, the capped hock lesion will rarely disappear.

Constriction of the Volar or Plantar Annular Ligament

Definition and Cause: The volar annular ligament (the hindleg version is called the plantar annular ligament) binds the fetlock joint. When an infection or a direct trauma such as a wirecut in that area starts to heal, this ligament may tighten. As it does so, it constricts the superficial flexor tendon.

Symptoms: The tendon sheath will be swollen, and the superficial flexor tendon will be thickened. From the lateral view, there will be a visible notching. The horse will be constantly lame, and this lameness will increase with work.

Treatment: Surgery is the only viable treatment: the ligament will have to be cut.

Contracted Heel

Definition and Causes: This is a condition in which the hoof, particularly the posterior portion of it, is more narrow than normal. Contracted heels occur most often in the front feet and commonly affect American Saddlebreds, Tennessee Walking Horses, Hackney Ponies, and other breeds in which the hoofs are grown to unnatural lengths. The long toes of such hoofs cause them to be out of balance. Also, the lack of frog pressure and weakening of the bars does not permit the hoof to act its part as a shock absorber. Dry feet, nails driven too far back in the hoof, poor trimming, improper shoeing, lack of exercise, or anything which inhibits the natural expansion of the heels can lead to contracted feet. Once contraction starts, the circulation to the heels is reduced, and the condition tends to get progressively worse. As the shock-absorbing ability of the hoof is impaired, the increased effect of concussion may in time make the horse lame.

Symptoms: Contracted heels are often accompanied by a "dished" sole. The frog also may be shriveled from lack of use. In most cases, of course, the contraction will be obvious upon inspection, especially if it occurs in one foot only.

Treatment: Although it may take only a few weeks for the horse to develop contracted feet, the condition may take more than a year to cure. In chronic cases, the coffin bone itself may become deformed, and the digital cushion atrophied.

Nearly all cases of contracted heels are accompanied by dry feet, and in such circumstances, the first step is to soak the feet; for this purpose wet burlap bags, mud holes, pails of water, anything wet may be used. Soak the feet for an hour or so each day. If your horse has a wet pasture to run around in, so much the better.

When the horse is shod, the object is to restore frog pressure, and get rid of the obstacles that hinder heel expansion. A bar shoe is one way to accomplish this; it gives the frog something to press upon. A T-shaped shoe will do the same thing, but in order for either of these to be effective, the hoofs must first be moist.

Contracted heels can almost always be avoided if proper hoof care and shoeing principles are followed.

Contracted Tendons

Definition and Causes: This condition occurs when for some reason the flexor tendons to the rear of the foreleg have become shorter than the cannon bone. The disorder can be either congenital or acquired, and can involve either one of the flexor tendons—deep or superficial—sometimes both. More uncommonly, the suspensory ligament is also contracted. How much the tendons are actually contracted is quite variable.

There are several established causes of contracted tendons. In some cases, foals are born with them, either because of a malformation of bone in the leg or spine, or because of crowding in the mare's uterus. This latter type will usually straighten out with time, if it is not too severe.

Another sort of contracture results from an injury, and occurs on one foot only. The muscles of the upper leg contract in an effort to alleviate the pain in joint movement.

A third type may be due to a deficiency of vitamin A or D or a calcium-phosphorus imbalance.

The most common sort, however, occurs in rapidly growing yearlings, particularly Thoroughbreds. The "contracture" is caused by the fact that the tendons have simply not managed to keep pace with the rapidly growing bones. In this case the foal has been getting too much phosphorus in his diet (grass hay may be the culprit here), and not enough calcium.

Symptoms: Mild cases resemble the stance of a "knee sprung" horse. The carpus will be knuckled forward and the horse will put his weight on the toe of the hoof. The pastern becomes more vertical also. In cases where only the superficial flexor tendon is contracted, the fetlock knuckles forward. If the deep flexor tendon is involved as well, the horse's heels may be lifted from the ground.

Treatment: In serious cases involving the deep flexor tendon, surgery may be necessary; in mild cases, proper shoeing, using a thick-heeled shoe, and time may be sufficient. Stall rest is important, and your veterinarian may wish to prescribe an anti-inflammation drug.

Corns

Definition and Causes: Corns are related to bruises, but they occur in one specific place—the angle between the bars and wall of the hoof. This area is in fact known as the seat of corn (see figure 7). Both sensitive and insensitive structures are involved. Corns most often occur in horses which are shod, and they usually develop on the inner part of the forefeet. They are actually the outward aspect of a bruise, but, on account of their location, are rather more difficult to treat. They can cause severe lameness, which worsens with exercise. Generally corns are caused by improper fitting of the shoes, or by shoes which fit originally but were left on too long. Heel calks seem to increase the occurrence of corns, as does cutting out the bars of the foot. Horses with contracted feet are often afflicted with chronic corns, and like bruises, corns are sometimes the forerunners of pedal osteitis.*

Symptoms: The appearance of a corn depends to a great extent upon how new it is; a simple dry corn is generally red, but darkens as it gets older. This is due to a staining of the horn by the breaking of the tiny blood vessels beneath.

Sometimes serum collects beneath to form what is called a moist corn; thin grayish white material may exude from it. If a corn becomes infected, the exudate will be a thick yellowish pus which can be an indication of serious trouble. Sometimes a fistula is even formed—a long tubelike structure with one opening at the corn and the other at the heel or coronet.

The horse will be mildly to severely lame, depending on the seriousness of the corn and its involvement with the deeper tissues.

Treatment: The shoes should be removed. The affected area should be pared with a hoof knife, and the feet soaked in warm water to soften the horn. If the horse is lame, a poultice should be applied to the foot. If the corn is supperating or infected, the foot should be soaked in an antiseptic.

When the horse is reshod, the wall and bars over the area may have to be lowered; all pressure must be removed from the seat of the corn. A bar or three-quarter shoe should be used until the horse is no longer lame. When regular shoes are put back on, they must be a little extra wide at the heels.

Curb

Definition and Causes: Curb is a hard swelling or bulge on the back leg about four inches below the point of hock. It results from a sprain or rupture of the plantar ligament, due to jumping, slipping, or over-exertion. Bad conformation, particularly sickle hocks and cow hocks, predispose to curb. Curb is seen in all breeds of horses, and young ones are especially susceptible. A hock affected by curb is somewhat weakened and may be susceptible to further injury.

Symptoms: The affected leg is semi-flexed, with the heel raised. There will be an intermittent lameness which, while in the acute stage, may increase with exercise. The lameness may totally disappear after some weeks. Sometimes the fetlocks make a cracking noise as the animal walks.

Treatment: The horse should be shod with wedge-heeled shoes to permit the foot to slide.

Dermatitis of the Pastern Area

Definition and Causes: There are a number of skin ailments affecting the pastern area, which are variously known as mud fever, grease, scratches, and cracked heel. If severe enough, any of them can cause lameness. These conditions occur mostly in cold damp weather and are aggravated by mud and dirt.

Symptoms: Often the skin at the back of the pastern area becomes inflamed and covered with scabs or a gray, greasy layer. The pasterns are often very tender, and the hair may fall out.

Treatment: The inflamed area should be cleaned and dried thoroughly. Excess hair should be clipped away, and zinc oxide ointment or antiseptic powder should be applied. If infection is present, topical antibiotics should be given.

Elbow Lameness

Definition and Causes: Real elbow lameness is neither common nor easy to diagnose. Generally it results from a fracture or restrictive arthritis (especially in older horses). It is often mistaken for shoulder lameness since the elbow and shoulder must work together.

Symptoms: The horse will nod his head quite noticeably when he is trotted. He will scarcely lift his hoof from the ground and when standing will rest the joint in a semi-flexed position.

Treatment: Rest.

(See also Capped Elbow and Radial Paralysis.)

Epiphysitis

Definition and Causes: This condition usually occurs in young, growing horses—in fact, in colts which are growing a bit too fast. Epiphysitis is, as its name suggests, an inflammation of the epiphysial plates, one of which is located at the lower end of the cannon bone, the other at the lower end of the radius. These plates change into bone as the colt grows older, the lower one between the ages of seven months and a year, the upper by the time the colt is two years old.

However, if the colt is too fat, his extra poundage can put a crushing force on this cartilage. Sometimes, too, a very toed-in conformation puts too great a stress on the inside leg. Quarter Horses, which sometimes have too heavy a body in relation to their small feet, are especially prone to this problem.

Symptoms: There will be a marked swelling at the site (almost always in the front legs), accompanied by a slight lameness.

Treatment: This inflammation is generally not too serious, since it occurs when the plates are starting to close, but it is a sign that the horse is growing too fast and should probably be put on a diet. Rest is also essential.

Fractures

Definition and Causes: A fracture is a break in the continuity of the bone. Fractures are of several sorts: simple, in which the skin is not broken; compound, in which the broken end of the bone punctures the skin; greenstick, in which one side of the bone is broken and the other only bent; and comminuted, where a number of bone splinters are found. Fortunately fractures do not often occur in the average riding horse. When they do occur, they are always very serious, and although the days are past when fractures automatically meant death for the horse, the high cost and doubtful prognosis make surgery inadvisable except for extremely valuable animals.

Fracture of the coffin bone: The coffin bone, although seldom broken, may fracture near its "wings." This is a difficult fracture to heal, and may not even show up on the X-ray for three or four days.

Symptom of Coffin Bone Fracture: Generally, the only symptom is severe lameness, and pain when the hoof is tapped with a hammer.

Fractures of the First and Second Phalanx: These bones above the foot are fractured more frequently than the coffin bone. Fractures of the first phalanx frequently occur in the hind leg, especially in cutting and reining horses, since these animals are subjected to sharp, twisting turns, which sometimes result in screwdriver fractures.

Symptoms of First and Second Phalanx Fractures: There is severe lameness of course, and the horse may refuse to put any weight at all on the limb. There will be a soft swelling, resembling an immense ringbone. The joint is often involved in such cases, making a normal recovery impossible.

Fractures of the Sesamoid Bones: The sesamoid bones are fractured with alarming frequency among race horses. These fractures arise from a combination of overexertion and fatigue. When the animal is tired, the flexors will not contract quickly enough and the extensor tendon can pull the toe of the foot forward by overextending the fetlock joint, thereby pulling the sesamoid bone forward against the phalanges.

Symptoms of Sesamoid Bone Fracture: The lameness resulting from this fracture is very pronounced and there will be swelling and pain.

Treatment: In all fracture cases, the veterinarian is the only one qualified to analyze the situation and prescribe treatment. The outlook is brightest for young animals with fractures that can be completely immobilized.

Gonitis (Stifle disease)

Definition and Causes: This is a catch-all term which includes a wide variety of disorders. In general, it refers to an inflammation of the stifle joint and may refer to an arthritis, a sprain, degeneration of the cartilage of the patella, fracture, or a number of other things.

Symptoms: These obviously depend upon the particular cause of the gonitis. Lameness varies with the severity of the gonitis; there will be a distention of the joint capsule. There may be a slightly positive response to the spavin test. Arthritic gonitis will be accompanied by swelling, heat, and pain.

Treatment: This, again, depends on the cause of the gonitis. If a sprain or trauma is suspected, the horse must be *completely confined* for at least a month. Injection of corticoids may be helpful.

Gravel

Definition and Causes: Gravel is allied to quittor as far as its general clinical appearance is concerned, but stems from a different cause, and usually affects a different part of the hoof. In gravel, a separation in the white line leads to an infection of the sensitive laminae, often by particles of manure or sand. The separation is thought to result (usually) from a sharp piece of gravel which is driven into the white line and opens a path in the hoof for manure and other infecting substances to enter. Unattended corns or sandcracks can lead to the same result.

Symptoms: Supporting leg lameness will be evident even before drainage occurs. There may be some heat in the hoof and/or fetlock region. Close examination of the hoof will reveal a black spot in the white line, which indicates the site of infection. In other cases, the occurrence of a pus pocket or abscess can be located with hoof testers.

Treatment: The opening must be enlarged so as to allow for drainage. Then apply tincture of iodine and bandage the hoof. Antibiotics and a tetanus antitoxin are called for, and the horse should be rested.

(See also: Quittor, Puncture Wounds, Separation.)

Joint Mice

Definition and Causes: This peculiar term refers to tiny pieces of cartilage or bone which accumulate at the border of a joint. The condition can be brought about by arthritis or a chip fracture, or it can be just one of those things—the cartilage just snaps.

Symptoms: The lameness is often intermittent, depending on whether or not a "mouse" is caught in the joint at that particular moment; if it is, the horse is very lame; if not, he seems sound.

Treatment: Surgery is the only effective treatment unless the mouse is extremely small, or it is not in direct interference with joint movement. Minor sequestra are sometimes reabsorbed into the blood.

Keratoma (Horn Tumor)

Definition and Causes: A horn tumor is a rare growth which appears at the toe of the hoof. It presses against the wall and sensitive laminae, but is usually benign (that is, it is unlikely to spread to surrounding tissues or to metastisize throughout the body). The tumor is made up of hard horn and is conelike in shape. Horn tumors develop slowly, and their cause is unknown at present—defects in the coronary band, sandcracks, and trauma have all been suggested.

Symptoms: There will be a bulge at the toe of the hoof. If you remove the shoe and pare the sole carefully at the point you will notice a round layer of horn which is different in texture from the surrounding tissue; this is the bottom of the keratoma.

Lameness will be present, but its development is slow.

Treatment: The veterinarian will probably perform a median neurectomy, an operation to cut the nerve which is responsible for the pain in the tumor region. Sometimes the tumor itself is cut out, but this is often useless, as the tumor is likely to return. Several months of rest are required after the operation. On the brighter side, much successful therapy is now being conducted using plastics.

Knee Lameness

Definition and Causes: Knee lameness can be of several types and has a variety of names: carpitis, Cherry's disease, knee spavin, popped knee, hygroma and hematoma. Knee lameness occurs both in heavy breeds (which sometimes tend to have narrow knees coupled with short forearms and upright shoulders) and in Thoroughbreds, whose carpal bones are subject to a great deal of shock.

An inflammation of the knee joint is most commonly known as a carpitis. It is caused by trauma and begins as a form of serous arthritis. If the arthritis becomes chronic, a spavin or osteoarthritis may result (see bone spavin) which is worse than that occurring in the hock region.

Symptoms: The knee is swollen and hard. Heat is present. The knee may be somewhat bent and may not be able to extend fully. When the animal moves, he will exhibit pain, and the leg will swing in an outside circle. The side of the hoof may strike the ground first. Lameness is intensified downhill.

Treatment: Rest is the best therapy, but unless the horse is young, the outlook is not favorable. Application of cold water and astringents may help in an acute case.

Laminitis (Founder)

Definition and Causes: Unfortunately, laminitis, or founder, is a very common and extremely painful disease of the horse's feet. It occurs in several forms, or types, which vary with the agent causing the condition. The results of all the different types are similar, however: destruction of the sensitive laminae of the hoof, and in severe cases a rotation of the coffin bone downward, sometimes even through the sole of the hoof.

What happens to produce this terrible condition? Although all the research has not yet been completed, the major steps are understood. In classical founder, which often affects a newly foaled mare that has failed to pass the afterbirth, or in horses that have overeaten or overdrunk, a toxin is formed by the body, generally in the intestine, from highly fermentable material such as new grass or grain, which is then absorbed into the blood stream. The toxin alters the blood circulation in the feet, resulting in a reduced supply to the corium and stagnation in other parts of the foot. Increased blood pressure causes intense pain, which is augmented by congestion and inflammation. A combination of the action of the toxins and the reduced nutrient supply to the growing areas of the hoof serve to weaken the laminae, allowing the coffin bone to rotate downward.

Ponies, especially fat and poorly conditioned ones, are susceptible to a type of founder known as "grass founder." It occurs usually in the spring after the rains, when the pastures are lush. Those pastures containing quantities of clover and alfalfa seem to be the most dangerous. This kind of founder often leaves a more or less permanent fatty deposit along the crest of affected animals.

Another type of founder, known as "road founder" seems to be primarily a result of concussion in overweight animals whose hoofs are left untrimmed. In this case the laminae actually tear due to the combination of concussion and extra weight on the hoofs. Allied to this sort is a laminitis which occurs unilaterally, or in one foot only. It results from a disease of the opposite foot which does not permit the horse to bear weight on that foot. The unaccustomed burden and lack of normal blood flow through the foot (which is often aggravated by the fact that the lame horse is frequently confined to a stall and unable to move about enough to improve circulation) starts the congestive process within the foot. Again, this horse is likely to have untrimmed feet, if only because he may be unable to stand on one leg long enough to have it done.

Laminitis has also occurred for no known reason. The cause may be hormonal, but no one is sure.

At any rate, once a horse has experienced a founder attack of whatever type, he becomes susceptible thereafter to future attacks.

Symptoms: The signs of laminitis are unmistakable. In a typical case both forefeet are held in front of the body in an effort to redistribute the weight towards the heels and the hind feet. Actually all four feet are generally affected, but the front feet show the most severe symptons since they bear the greatest part of the animal's weight. In very severe cases, the animal will be lying down, or if he can stand at all, all four legs will be placed underneath the body.

The hoof will generally be warm to the touch, from the sole to the coronary band, and the arteries of the lower leg may pulsate noticeably. Sometimes pain is the only symptom.

If untreated, chronic laminitis will result. In the chronic form, the hoof itself changes shape in response to the interior pressures of the laminae. The sole of the hoof drops and is protected by abnormal amounts of flaky material. The wall of the hoof becomes dished due to the sinking of the coronet and the front wall is wrinkled. Frequently these rings will remain throughout the life of the horse. (In severe cases, the front wall may actually begin to curl up, like a pair of Turkish slippers.) Because of the persistent inflammation, the coffin bone itself may undergo a demineralization, called pedal osteitis.*

Treatment: Emergency measures, designed to reduce the acute congestion within the hoof, are essential. Your veterinarrian may even bleed the hoof at the toe, or he may inject adrenaline or antihistamines. Before he arrives, put ice water on the hoofs; if Claude can be persuaded to stand in a bucket of it, so much the better.

Your vet may wish to administer mineral oil as a laxative and to help prevent any more absorption of the toxins which led to the attack. Tranquilizers and an analgesic, anti-inflammatory drug may also be prescribed.

As soon as the acute stage has passed, the real hope lies in the shoeing. The basic principle is to relieve the weight and pressure on the toe, where the most serious damage has occurred (since the laminae are longer there) and where there is likely to be a separation at the white line. All the excess horn tissue must be rasped away; the heels should be lowered as far as possible. This is an attempt to place the coffin bone back in proper alignment. Next a wide webbed (sometimes a bar or saucer) shoe with a pad to increase the low heel effect is applied. This trimming and shoeing must be done every four weeks if the attempt to restructure the natural hoof shape is to succeed.

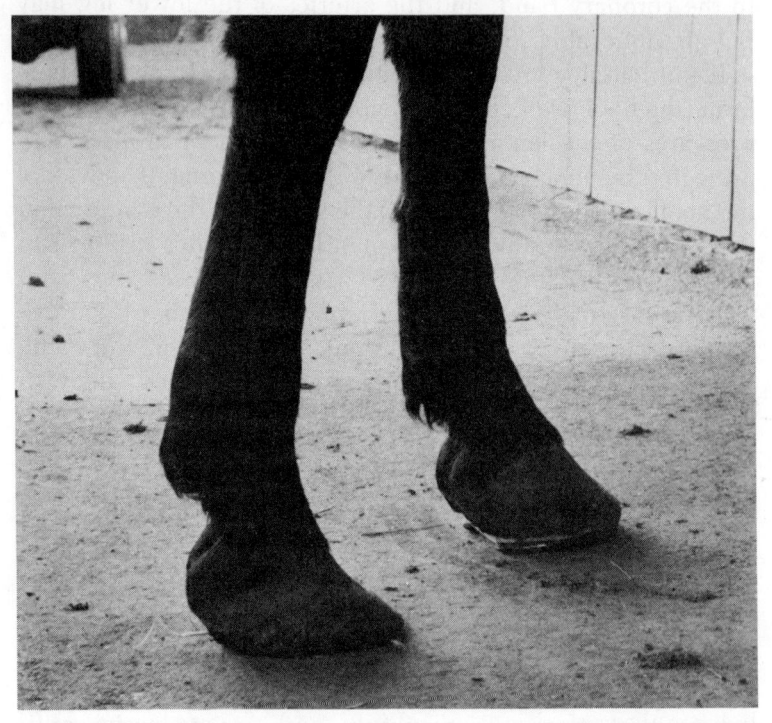

A foundered hoof restored to nearly normal by careful trimming and use of a leather pad. Note the founder lines visible on the right hoof, which has not yet been trimmed.

Founder, although dreadful, can in large measure be avoided by the owner who feeds his horse reasonably, keeps his horse's hoofs trimmed, and does not gallop down the road on a barefoot horse. Remember that the eating of young, spring grass is most likely to lead to founder.

Navicular Disease

Definition and Causes: Navicular disease is one of the mystery diseases of the horse world. Some veterinarians believe navicular is overdiagnosed, while others think it goes unrecognized too often. Some authorities consider the entire condition a misnomer, while others claim to be uncertain even as to what the disease actually is—inflammation of the bone, degeneration of the bone, or neither. Matters are not helped by the fact that X-rays fail to confirm a large percentage of diagnosed navicular trouble. It is true that navicular is being diagnosed more and more, but whether this is a real increase, or the result of more accurate diagnoses (or, as some authorities contend, a fad) is not presently known. Many regard the problem as hereditary, but this is probably true only in the sense that the navicular-prone conformation—narrow, contracted, upright feet—is inherited. Since concussion plays a major role in the development of the condition, horses with upright pasterns and shoulders are more susceptible.

The disease probably begins as a bursitis* of the navicular bursa, which lies between the deep flexor tendon and the navicular bone. Normally the deep flexor tendon glides over the posterior aspect of this bone, which acts like a fulcrum for it. This tendon gives a good deal of support to the navicular bone, but at the same time it puts quite a lot of pressure on both bone and bursa, particularly at the point in the stride when the foot acts as a support column for the horse's body as it passes over it.

The disease is an insidious one which begins first in the cartilage and tendon; then lesions occur on the surface of the bone itself. The inflammation of the bone encourages it to form osteophytes, or bone "spurs." The navicular bone itself generally becomes pitted with "craters," but of course these can be seen, if at all, only on the X-ray. Remember that navicular disease, in its early stages at least, is not an arthritis; it does not affect the joint surface of the bone, but begins as a bursitis—that is, it affects the tendon aspect of the bone.

The causes of navicular disease vary from poor conformation, concussion, poor trimming practices, or likely enough, a combination of the three: anything which increases the normal amount of pressure of the deep flexor tendon against the navicular bone. For example, many farriers mistakenly trim the heels too low in a horse with upright pasterns in an effort to create an "ideal" hoof angle of 50 degrees. This of course changes the horse's natural axis and puts even more pressure on the navicular bone. Show jumpers and rodeo event horses, for instance, are commonly afflicted with navicular trouble.

Symptoms: Usually both front feet are affected (although often one more so than the other), which increases the difficulty in diagnosis. Remember that a horse hurting in both front feet often seems to be less lame than if only one were affected. The lameness will probably appear very gradually, and will be intermittent or light. It will be most obvious the day *after* the horse is worked. The horse may "point" and show an alteration in gait: a short pottery stride or perhaps a gingerly "shuffling motion." This often leads the owner to think it has a shoulder problem. The lameness should increase if the horse is turned in tight circles. The horse may also tend to "screw" or pivot on his front feet. Usually the toe of the most affected foot will show excessive wear, since the horse tries to land on his toes to keep weight off the painful area. This in turn many cause the horse both to stumble and to develop bruises in the toe area.

Pressure applied in the center of the frog with hoof testers may produce pain. Many horses with navicular disease have contracted heels also, which of course affects the proper blood supply to the foot, and may be regarded as a contributing cause.

As the disease progresses, the hoof tends to become very blocky, short in the toe region and deep in the heel. This "self-defense" mechanism relieves much of the pressure from the navicular bone. In advanced cases, too, the "navicular waist" often appears—the hoof wall is wider at the top and bottom than it is in the middle. In addition, the hoof wall may be dished.

The most effective diagnostic tools of all, the nerve block and the X-ray, can only be used by your veterinarian.

Treatment: Real navicular disease is incurable; the treatment is aimed mainly at (1) reducing pressure on the navicular bone and bursa and (2) relieving pain.

Cortisone injections and anti-inflammatory drugs like Butazolidin are commonly employed, but the relief granted is only temporary. A posterior digital neurectomy (where a section of the nerve is removed) is sometimes performed, but this is an expensive solution which can have complications. The loss of feeling in the area may cause the horse to overextend his foot and rupture the deep digital flexor tendon.

In most cases, navicular symptoms can be relieved by therapeutic shoeing methods. These consist of shortening the toe and raising the heel to assist in proper breakover of the foot and paring the sole more than usual to make up for the lack of frog pressure. The horse should then be shod with a rocker toe shoe with swelled heels to maintain the correct breakover. Leather pads and silicone are also used.

Many cases of navicular disease could be prevented by less enthusiastic efforts to "correct" a horse's natural hoof angle, and by a greater respect for the *normal* use of the animal.

Osselets (Little Bones)

Definition and Causes: These are osteophytes which form in the anterior part of the fetlock joint. They are caused by an inflammation of the joint capsule resulting from damage to the articular cartilage on the front of the cannon bone and first phalanx. This is in fact a form of traumatic arthritis, and the osteophytes can become quite large.

Concussion is the most important fact in the occurrence of osselets, particularly in the young horse just beginning his racing training. Direct trauma, pulling away of part of the joint capsule, may also be a cause.

Symptoms: The horse will be lame, and there is heat and swelling over the front of the fetlock joint. This swelling will be fairly soft and quite painful. There also will be an increase in synovial fluid forming a wind puff,* and the joint capsule is thickened. This condition will persist. If the horse has developed osselets on both front legs, he will move with a short choppy gait.

Treatment: Corticoids are useful, but the horse must be rested as well or osteoarthritis may develop in the joint. After the calcium deposits have formed, the horse may be serviceably sound for years.

Pedal Osteitis

Definition and Causes: Pedal osteitis refers to an inflammation of the coffin bone. This inflammation leads to a demineralization or roughening of the bone, and the consequent production of new bone growth in the area. Generally, only one foot is involved, and the condition is associated with corns, chronic bruising, and laminitis. The vascular system is often involved and there may be congestion in the hoof.

Pedal osteitis used to be most common in draft and cavalry animals, but nowadays many Thoroughbreds, whose soles are pared too thin, are affected.

Symptoms: The horse will be tender on his feet and tend to "go short." The lameness may at first be intermittent, but when it is present, will show up at all gaits. The condition worsens if the horse is run over gravel. There may be some heat in the foot, and the horse may wince if the sole is tapped with a hammer.

Treatment: The disease is irreversible, but if the horse is turned out on soft pasture for several months and then shod with wide-webbed or bar shoes, he may improve a great deal.

Puncture Wounds

Definition and Causes: A puncture wound is one which is deeper than it is wide. This may seem a trivial distinction (and I wouldn't at all advise going about with a tape measure in case you're not certain), but it is important to know why puncture wounds in particular are so dangerous. It is because they allow bacteria to become trapped within the body and to grow. Tetanus bacteria, especially, which live in manure piles, are likely culprits.

Puncture wounds are caused by a depressingly large array of objects, but the most common is the nail. (It makes no difference, by the way, whether or not the nail is rusty.) A puncture wound most often occurs during the shoeing process, when the nail is driven inside the white line and penetrates to the sensitive tissues. The infection then develops in these and the vascular parts. If the nail is more than one inch long, it may, if it enters the hoof at the right point and angle, puncture the coffin or navicular bone. Small-headed nails sometimes even disappear into the hoof to confuse the issue further, but puncture wounds are such a common occurrence they should always be suspected in any foot lameness. Therefore, even if you see no nail, it may be wise to pare a very thin layer from the sole and frog with a hoof knife to expose a possible nail head. The softer frog is particularly concealing. Remember too that the original cause of the puncture may be missing. Don't give up looking until you are sure that there is no nail involved.

Symptoms: Sometimes these take a day or so to develop, as pus accumulates within the wound. (If the nail is still in the hoof, the horse will refuse to put his foot down at all.) Although difficult to diagnose, there is generally some tenderness in the area, which is intensified if tapped with a hammer. If the pus accumulates to any degree, the horse may be hot and blowing, signs of great distress. Swelling may occur around the fetlock, especially in the later stages. If the wound is in the toe region, the horse may tend to land farther back on his heels than is normal; if the puncture is towards the heels, he will land toe first. Sometimes there are visible cracks or spots which may be seen if the hoof is scrubbed clean.

Treatment: The nail hole should be enlarged with a hoof knife to allow for drainage. A poultice also will soften the horn and reduce pressure by assisting the drainage. The wound must be kept very clean while it is healing. It should be disinfected with tincture of iodine and a tetanus toxoid should be given.

Once the drainage has stopped, the horse should be shod, using a leather pad packed with oakum and pine tar to seal the wound. This is essential, especially if the coffin bone should be exposed.

Although puncture wounds cannot always be prevented, their occurrence can be greatly minimized by keeping the environs of the horse as free from trash as possible. In addition, checking your horse's feet each day (particularly the first few days after shoeing) will increase your chances of catching the puncture early.

It should not be necessary to add that if your horse should **develop a puncture wound, he must be rested until it is healed.**

Quittor

Definition and Causes: Quittor is an extremely painful chronic infection within the hoof involving the lateral cartilage of the coffin bone. The cartilage becomes necrosed, or dead, and the material drains through a sinus opening in the coronary band, since this is the path of least resistance for the pressure which builds up inside the hoof. It generally occurs in the front feet, and in the past commonly affected draft horses, who sometimes stepped on themselves while pulling heavy loads.

Quittor is usually caused by a direct trauma such as tread wounds, interference, or a puncture wound in the sole of the hoof. An abscess or wire cut near the coronary band can also lead to quittor.

Symptoms: There will be heat, pain, and swelling at the coronary band, if the pus has not yet been discharged from the lateral cartilages. Even if no pus has yet appeared, the pus pocket can often be located with hoof testers or a hammer.

Lameness is present, particularly in the acute stages when the pus is building up. Sidebone, the ultimate result of quittor, is sometimes present also.

Treatment: The necrotic cartilage must be removed, generally by surgery. The area around the pus pocket should be kept clipped and bandaged. Fortunately quittor is becoming rare today.

(See also Gravel.)

Radial Paralysis or Dropped Elbow

Definition and Causes: This problem is not actually in the elbow at all, but due to a paralysis of the radial nerve. This thick nerve runs in front of the long head of the triceps and goes into the muscle-spinal groove of the humerus lying over the brachialis muscle. It provides sensation to the extensors of the elbow, knee, fetlock, pastern, and coffin joints. The radial nerve can be paralyzed by a kick on the humerus, which is why spirited colts are sometimes affected.

Symptoms: They arise quite suddenly. The horse will stand with the knee and fetlock semiflexed. In complete radial paralysis the horse will be completely unable to advance the leg. When the horse is backed, the bad leg will drag after it. The elbow will be in a lowered position.

Treatment: Nothing can be done, but it is possible the nerve may repair itself. Allow about six weeks for this. If no improvement is made by then, the horse will probably not get better.

Ridge Lesion

Definition and Causes: This disorder occurs deep inside the fetlock joint and is not easily detected. A ridge lesion is an erosion of the ridge which separates the anterior from the posterior half of the cannon bone joint surface. It occurs when the fetlock joint dorsiflexes too far; the sesamoid bones get pulled over this ridge, which acts as a fulcrum. The sesamoid bones press and vibrate against the joint, causing articular damage. Ridge lesions are caused by overwork, and poor shoeing.

Treatment: Rest is essential; the return to work must be very gradual.

Ringbone

Definition and Causes: Like many other lamenesses, ringbone can more accurately be considered a condition than an actual disease. It is a bony enlargement (or deposit) which can occur anywhere in the area of the pastern. This bony outgrowth is commonly referred to as an "exostosis." If this exostosis occurs fairly high up in the pastern (near the lower end of the first phalanx), it is known as high ringbone (figure 33a): if it occurs lower down (near the bottom of the second phalanx), it is called low ringbone (figure 33b).

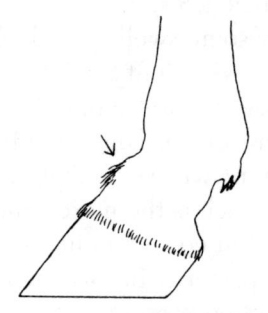

Figure 33a. High ringbone.

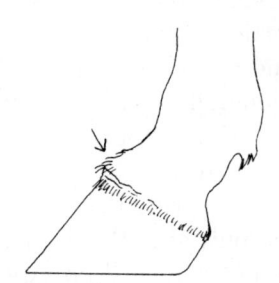

Figure 33b. Low ringbone.

Ringbone, whether high or low, is of two sorts: articular—that is, involving a joint surface; or non-articular. Articular ringbone is of course more serious, and often results from arthritis* in the area. The inflammation which can accompany arthritis encourages the development of the osteophytes or bone spurs; these sometimes even fuse the joint together and thus immobilize it. Articular ringbone more often occurs in racehorses than in other types of horses; the first phalanx rotates too far on the second phalanx at high speeds, which puts excessive strain on one part of the joint and begins to destroy the cartilage.

Non-articular ringbone is not serious in itself if it does not inhibit joint and tendon action, but it can lead to the articular type, since there will unavoidably be some increased resistance to joint flexion.

Ringbone can appear in either the fore or hind feet, but is more common in the former. Horses of all ages are affected. The cause of ringbone is most often attributed to trauma, but there may be a genetic influence involved. Too low heels and uneven trimming have also been singled out, as have Vitamin A and calcium and phosphorus deficiencies.

Symptoms: Early cases may show some swelling and a little heat in the region. Marked lameness is evident at all gaits, but the horse may improve with exercise, or "warm out of it." (In later stages, the lameness, when present, is constant.) In the non-articular form of ringbone, there will very likely be no lameness at all. In high ringbone, which is the more common and generally less serious type, a firm convex bulge will develop on the upper surface of the pastern. In low ringbone, the characteristic buttress foot* may be present. It should be noted, however, that in most instances these external signs appear only after the damage has been done, and the horse at this point may well be experiencing no discomfort.

Treatment: After a period of complete rest, the most useful treatment is proper shoeing of the affected animal; in cases of high ringbone, full roller-motion shoes are employed to aid the stiffened joint movement. Another shoeing objective is to help relax the tendons where they are stretched over the oseophytes. If the deposits are mainly on the front, thin heeled shoes are used; if on the rear, thick heeled shoes are called for.

Sandcracks

Definitions and Causes: A sandcrack is an unsoundness which can occur in any area of the hoof—toe, quarter, or heel. It is most common in the quarters, where the wall is thinner than at the toe, and usually occurs on the inside of the front feet, where concussion is greatest. (Cracks in the hind feet often occur at the toe.) Some cracks, which usually begin at the lower border of the hoof, are very shallow, except perhaps at the point of origin. They are usually the result of direct trauma from concussion or injury and are sometimes called fissures. These cracks are not in themselves very serious, but can lead to a genuine sandcrack if not treated. Another very peculiar type of sandcrack is called a cleft, which is a horizontal, rather than a vertical, fissure. Clefts usually result from an injury to the coronary band, as does a true sandcrack.

Severe hoof cracks. The horizontal lines reveal an attempt to halt the further progression of the cracks, but the deep central crack needs immediate attention.

Sandcracks begin at the coronary band and work downward.

A predisposing cause of cracks is a dry or shelly hoof, a condition which can arise from anything from excessive rasping of the hoof to a deficiency in thyroid secretion. If a hoof is not trimmed regularly, the growth of the hoof wall will cause it to split and form a fissure. Poorly fitting shoes or too-short heels can also lead to cracks.

Symptoms: Besides the obvious and visible appearance of a crack, the horse may become lame, for one of two reasons:

First, the crack may become infected; in this instance the lameness will be extreme. Generally, a swelling of the coronet over the crack will indicate this condition.

Second, a deep sandcrack may involve the sensitive tissues. As the horse walks, this crack will open and close in response to pressure. Whether the crack opens or closes as the hoof strikes the ground depends upon exactly where in the hoof it is located. As the crack closes, it will pinch the laminae beneath, causing considerable pain.

Treatment: The sandcrack will not grow together by itself, since the outer horn tissue is dead. Until the hoof grows out (which will take approximately eight months) the crack must be immobilized in some way, so that the new horn, as it begins to grow out, will not crack.

There are several ways to accomplish this. (Before any attempt is made to repair the crack, however, it should be cleaned of dirt and grit. If infection is present, pack some cotton soaked with tincture of iodine into the crack. Antibiotics may also be required.) Formerly—and it is a method still used by many farriers—the technique was to rivet the edges of the crack together by driving a horseshoe nail across the crack and clinching it at both ends. This was repeated at one-inch intervals along the length of the crack.

Another method, especially with toe cracks, is to shoe the horse with clips at each side of the crack (see Figure 34), or to use a barshoe.

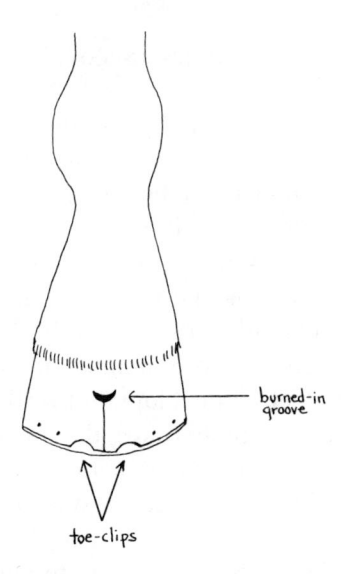

Figure 34. Correcting for sandcracks.

In the earlier stages of the development of a crack, it can sometimes be prevented from extending any farther by making a groove in the hoof wall with a hoof groover, hoof saw, or a flat firing iron at red heat. This groove can be either horizontal or V-shaped.

Nowadays hoof cracks are also treated by use of plastics—dental epoxy, fiberglass, and special patented hoof repair material are all in use. First, of course, the crack must be cleaned very thoroughly, as the plastic will seal it (and anything in it) completely. The advantage of using plastic is that it prevents subsequent infection of the sensitive tissue and also that the job looks much more cosmetically pleasing than the older methods. It should be noted, however, that the heat which the plastics generate can be harmful to the hoof tissue beneath. The hoof should be kept as dry as possible to ensure that the plastic stays put.

Separation (Seedy Toe)

Definition and Causes: This condition represents a destruction of the white line. It occurs most often at the toe of the hoof, where the laminae are longer and consequently weaker. Sometimes an actual cavity forms in this softer tissue, which is filled with a dark caseous substance. This material is really broken up horn and may be infected. The cavity is conical in shape and may extend to the top of the hoof.

The cause of seedy toe is unknown, but blows, puncture wounds, and defective development of the horn tissue have all been suggested. Sometimes the overuse of an unshod horse may also lead to inflammation and separation of the laminae, since the pressure can result in a migration of horn tissue.

Symptoms: The horse may be quite lame, but other signs may be difficult to detect. Tapping with a hammer on the hoof wall makes a hollow sound. Careful inspection of the sole of the hoof may reveal a black line which indicates the separation.

Treatment: The cavity must be disinfected with iodine and filled with cotton or oakum and pine tar. The wall near the area should be lowered, and a leather pad applied before a shoe is put on to avoid pressure at the point of contact with the shoe.

(See also Gravel.)

Sesamoiditis

Definition and Causes: Sesamoiditis is a painful inflammation of the sesamoid bones or of the sesamoid sheath of the flexor tendon. It can be caused by jumping or sharply reining back a little too often—anything, in fact, which causes undue strain to the fetlock joint. Thus it is most common among hunters, steeplechasers, and flat racers.

What happens is that the attachments of the suspensory ligament to the sesamoid bones are torn by strain. The resulting inflammation affects the sesamoid bones usually as an ulceration of their joint surfaces. The metacarpophalangeal sheath (through which the flexor tendons glide) becomes distended also. This swelling is sometimes called tenosynovitis and can occur in a number of ailments.

Symptoms: There will be a sudden onset of well-marked lameness which increases with work. The fetlock will be swollen at the back and there may be a good deal of heat present. The whole area will be quite sensitive, and the horse will flinch when the fetlock is pressed. New windpuffs* may be present also. The horse may resist starting to move, and will likely hold the affected fetlock flexed with the heel raised. Caution: if the horse does not evidence pain when the area is pressed, it is probably not sesamoiditis. Look lower down—at the hoof.

Treatment: It is wise to have X-rays taken in any case of suspected sesamoiditis, since a fracture may be present. If the suspensory ligament is involved, no treatment is really very satisfactory, but in any event the horse should be rested and an attempt made to reduce the inflammation by corticosteroid therapy. Cold water and elastic adhesive bandages may be beneficial. In acute cases casting may be necessary.

When shoeing, lower the toe and keep the heels high. A special shoe can be applied with a bar welded across the back to raise the heels about one-half inch from the ground. The toe of this shoe should be rolled to relieve strain on the ligament.

Shoulder Lameness

Definition and Causes: It is possible, though not likely, that the shoulder may become injured through a wrench or fall. The average horseowner blames many vague lamenesses on the shoulder—generally on sore muscles. He is almost always wrong. Horses seldom have anything wrong with their shoulders. But, in case your horse is one of those who do, shoulder lameness is indicated by the following:

Symptoms: The horse will lift his head sharply as his leg is brought forward. Depending on how sore he is, he will be reluctant or very reluctant to raise his foot high enough to clear the ground. Stumbling will be frequent—not when he sets his foot down, as in foot lameness, but when he attempts to pick it up. He will move with a characteristic "three-cornered" gait. His lameness does not improve on soft ground as in hoof lameness; it may even get worse. And shoulder lameness markedly increases when the horse goes uphill. In a severe case the horse cannot trot at all. There, now you have it. Shoulder lameness signs are quite distinct really, and you will probably never see them.

Sidebone

Definition and Causes: Sidebone is simply the name for the condition in which the lateral cartilages ossify. This hardening generally begins at the coffin bone and spreads outward, so that it is at first indiscernable. Sidebone is somewhat serious since when it occurs the proper function of the lateral cartilages—to aid in the expansion of the foot—is hindered or even made impossible. Since the cartilages also help pump the venous blood in the foot, circulation troubles can develop. When sidebone does occur, it is usually the outside lateral cartilage which ossifies first; especially in base-narrow horses. It nearly always occurs in both front feet at once, and the hind feet are rarely affected.

Sidebone does not generally cause lameness itself, although it often occurs with contraction and a concurrent ringbone.

The causes of sidebone are not agreed upon at present. Concussion, injuries, contracted heels, heredity and sandcracks have all been named. Sidebone occurs most often in draft horses, mules, Quarter Horses, and heavy hunters, while it is quite rare in Thoroughbreds.

Symptoms: Sidebone is hard to detect in its earlier stages, which occur inside the hoof, and later lameness may or may not be present. If there is lameness, the horse may "point" and tend to land toe first. There will also be heat over the cartilages. Later on, sidebone can be tested for by trying to bend the cartilages inward, as can be done in a normal foot. Ossified cartilage will not permit this. In the later stages of sidebone, there may be a chronic swelling below the knee due to insufficient blood return.

Treatment: In the early stages, rest the horse and apply cold packs to reduce the inflammation. In a really acute case, the veterinarian may prescribe corticosteroids or phenylbutazone. When the horse is shod, the shoes should be rocked, and pads used to act as shock absorbers, to partially take over the function of the lateral cartilages.

Spavin

There are two forms of true spavin (bog spavin* is a misnomer): bone (or jack) spavin, and occult spavin.

Bone Spavin

Definition and Causes: This is a bony enlargement, similar to ringbone in nature, on the inner, lower side of the hock. It involves the distal bone of the tarsus and the head of the cannon bone. Bone spavin is actually an osteoarthritis. It may be due to bad conformation, especially cow hocks and sickle hocks. Those horses used on hard roads are also subject to spavin, and overexertion of young horses also claims its share of victims. Mineral imbalance, too, may be at fault. Bone spavin is always serious—just how serious depends on the exact location of the lesion.

Occult Spavin

Definition and Causes: Occult (which means "hidden") spavin, like bone spavin is an arthritis, but there is no bony enlargement apparent. Its causes are the same as those leading to bone spavin.

Symptoms: The horse may be lame for quite a long period of time before any outward lesion is visible (if it ever is.) This lameness may be intermittent. The spavin test, as described on page 00, is the prime indicator of the presence of spavin. The lameness will be much more severe after the leg is held flexed.

In bone spavin the lameness will improve with exercise, especially in mild cases. In occult spavin, the horse will be continuously lame. He will react positively to the spavin test, although perhaps not quite so positively as in bone spavin. (Be sure to conduct the test on both legs.) Turning the horse with a lame leg outside increases the lameness. Later the typical exostosis will appear; it will vary in size from case to case, and most often occur on the inner side of the hock.

Horses with severe bone spavin may develop navicular trouble because of the extra weight put on the front feet.

Treatment: Rest is vital in the early stages (in occult spavin this will be for at least six months). When the horse is shod, the toe should be lowered and the heels raised (a wedge heel is good for this). Toe clips may be necessary.

Sometimes surgery will achieve results; at other times the natural or encouraged ankylosis (crookedness) of the bones is desirable.

Splints

Definition and Causes: Actually a form of periostitis, splints are a common condition of horses under five years of age and are not permanently damaging unless they happen to interfere with the working of the suspensory ligament—the so-called peg splint. (This occurs when the splint forms on the inside of the splint bone and is a serious and permanent condition.) Splints most often occur between the cannon and the splint bone (the large and small metacarpals) on the inside of the front leg or, more rarely, on the outside of the hind leg. In the young horse, these splint bones are attached to the cannon bone by ligaments only. If the suspensory or interosseous ligament (which literally means "between the bones") is torn, there is acute inflammation which will lead to the formation of new bone growth (exostoses). The new bone acts as a wedge to prevent further tearing. Splints happen because the inside splint bone is pushed downwards and backwards as weight is applied, and excessive strain causes the tearing of the ligament.

Other predisposing factors include poor conformation (toed-in or toed-out) and mineral imbalance, particularly too much phosphorus in relation to calcium, which occurs as a result of overfeeding of bran. If there is not enough calcium in the diet, the parathyroid glands will produce a hormone which draws calcium from the bones to maintain the normal amount in the blood stream. And it strips the calcium first from the outer layers of bone where the ligaments are attached. Thus the splint bones are the first to be affected.

Symptoms: The horse will be lame (often intermittently) before the swelling becomes noticeable. The swelling itself, located between the splint and cannon bone, will be hot and painful on pressure.

The horse will often be sound at the walk but trot lame. The lameness increases with exercise and is worse on hard ground and downhill.

To find a splint, flex the carpus and run your thumb in the space between the cannon and splint bones from the knee down to the nodule. Most splints occur in the distal third of the splint bone, about one-half way down the cannon bone. The splint can be as small as a pea, or very large. (Like a splinter in your finger, the smaller it is, the more painful it can be.)

Treatment: Rest is the best therapy, but it is well to allow the horse freedom in his field. If the horse is worked when splints are forming, large exostoses may develop, which may have to be surgically removed (although if treated early enough while still soft, they may be encouraged to be reabsorbed into the system). Injections of corticoids are also sometimes used.

Sprain and Strain

Definitions and Causes: These terms are often used interchangeably. Some authorities consider a sprain to be the *tearing* of a muscle, ligament, tendon, or the sheaths which support them, while the term strain refers to the *overstretching* of the structure. Other authorities use the word sprain to refer primarily to injury to the ligaments and strain to damage of the muscles and tendons. It is well for the horse owner to be acquainted with both usages. In any event, the cause of both sprain and strain is excessive force. The structure then becomes tense, and gives way—generally at one of its attachments. If it should pull a portion of the bone with it, it is called a fracture sprain. Although a sprain can affect any ligament, we will consider here only sprains of the suspensory ligament and flexor tendon.

The overstress most often occurs when fatigue sets in; the muscles tire and lose some of their contractile ability. The force is then taken up by the inelastic tendons, which will tear, as they are not able to withstand the force applied. Although some sprains (of the subcarpal ligament, for instance) can occur from sharp wrenches, sprains of the suspensory ligament and flexor tendons are due primarily to overexertion. Sometimes in a sprain the periosteum is torn and/or inflamed. As a result, new bone is formed.

Sprain of the suspensory ligament occurs most often in Thoroughbreds, usually with accompanying injury of the flexor tendons. The sprain generally occurs at the branches of the ligament where they attach to the upper part of the sesamoid bones, when the fetlock is dorsiflexed while the horse is at a gallop. This type of sprain results from the fact that the exhausted flexor tendons can no longer help support the pastern and fetlock. Uneven trimming of the hoofs increases the chance for sprain.

Symptoms: New sprains are puffy and swollen and are painful to the touch. Later, the diffuse swelling of the sprain becomes more defined. The area will usually be warm. Sprains do not pit when pressed with a finger. If the swelling does pit, it is more likely to be a tenosynovitis of some sort.

Sprains also cause lameness. If the suspensory ligament and flexor tendons are involved, the animal will rest with his knee flexed and the heels of the foot resting off the ground. Even in motion the fetlock will not descend to its normal level. In long standing cases, there may be a resulting contracted tendon.

Treatment: When sprain first occurs, apply a pressure bandage and administer cold water, which will help reduce the swelling. If the injury is not discovered until some time after it occurs, hot packs should be used.

Rest is mandatory, and massaging the affected areas will help. Blistering and firing are sometimes employed.

Stringhalt

Definition and Causes: Also called springhalt, this nervous disorder is probably due to a dysfunction in the spinal cord. It may affect one or both back legs.

Symptoms: The hindleg will jerk upward while the horse is in motion. The amount of flexion depends upon the severity of the condition. Stringhalt is particularly noticeable when the horse is turning or backing, and is often worse in cold weather. The condition improves with exercise, but unfortunately worsens as the animal grows older.

Treatment: Surgery is sometimes effective; part of the lateral extensor tendon (where it passes over the hock) is removed.

Sweeny

Definitions and Causes: Sweeny is a term which refers to atrophied muscles, generally in the shoulder region. This degeneration of tissue is caused by damage to the suprascapular nerve (which supplies the supraspinatus and infraspinatus muscles). Often a direct blow to the shoulder is the original cause, and sweeny and bicipital bursitis may occur together. Slipping and pulling heavy loads can also be responsible.

Symptoms: The shoulder joint appears prominent due to the atrophy of the surrounding muscles. Sometimes, as the horse moves forward, the shoulder seems to pop outward as the horse puts weight on the leg. The stride will be shortened.

Treatment: None is effective. Either the nerve will repair itself or it won't.

Thoroughpin

Definition and Causes: Thoroughpin is a form of tenosynovitis; that is, it is a swelling of the tarsal sheath through which the flexor tendons glide. It occurs most often in young horses with straight hocks, and in fact is due to a strain of the flexor tendons as they pass over the hock.

Symptoms: Thoroughpin is easiest to see when looked at from behind. There will be a bulge (usually more prominent on one side than the other). If you press this bulging side of the thoroughpin, it will reappear on the other side. The lesion occurs right above the point of hock, about two inches in front of the Achilles tendon. It generally appears in one leg only. In an acute case, the horse may be lame, and the thoroughpin will be hot, soft, and puffy. Later it will neither cause lameness nor be painful.

Treatment: Cold compresses, rest, and wrapping may be helpful in an acute case; chronic forms need no treatment.

Thrush

Definition and Causes: Thrush is simply a form of hoof rot. (There does not seem to be a more attractive synonym.) It is the most common problem of the hoof, and luckily is both treatable and, in general, preventable. It affects the frog of the hoof (and its clefts both in the middle and to the sides) and is caused by a yeast with the name of Spherophourus necrophorus. Spherophourus necrophorus loves a damp airless environment such as that found in manure heaps, especially if the manure happens to be heaped into your horse's hoofs. If allowed to remain in the hoof, sooner or later it will set busily to work removing the frog. Remember that your horse needs this resilient pad as an auxiliary blood pump and shock absorber.

For some reason, certain horses seem prone to thrush, even though their hoofs and stalls are kept scrupulously clean. One partial explanation might be that some horses exude excess amounts of material from their "sweat glands" deep in the cleft of the frog. The yeast seem to be particularly fond of this material.

Symptoms: The most noticeable sign of thrush is its odor. This is just awful, and once you smell it, you won't forget it. (Actually an abscess smells considerably worse, but you won't forget that either.) Also there is a blackish exudate from the cleft of the frog; the frog itself may be raw and tender. In severe cases, the horse will be lame.

Treatment: First clean the hoof thoroughly and wash it out with a mild disinfectant, then allow the hoof to dry. In most cases a patented thrush remedy can then be applied. Those containing copper naphthalate are generally effective. Severer cases may require the services of a farrier who will trim away the infected parts of the frog. For very severe cases, when the disease has penetrated quite far into the hoof, a tetanus shot or antibiotics for systemic necrophorus infections may be needed.

Thrush, by the way, can be contagious, so be sure not to use the same hoof pick on a sound horse after cleaning the feet of one with thrush. Disinfect everything.

Tying Up Syndrome

Definition and Causes: This painful condition seems to be a mild, related form of azoturia. It generally appears following great exertion following a rest when the grain ration was not reduced. Renal damage is not present.

Symptoms: The horse will be stiff; the hind legs will not flex normally. Pressure over the kidney region will produce pain.

Treatment: Walk the horse for at least half an hour.

Upward Fixation of the Patella

Definition and Causes: This condition is sometimes called luxation of the patella, but this term is a misnomer, since upward fixation is not, strictly speaking, a dislocation. The patella "catches" on the trochlear process of the tibia. When this occurs the ligaments may be stretched so that it recurs more easily. Long, straight legs are prone to this disorder, especially in animals under two years old. Sometimes the problem can become chronic, leading to an inflammation of the joint—gonitis.*

Symptoms: When the patella is locked, the horse's hind leg will be extended to the rear in a characteristic position, as if it were being dragged. The horse will move forward with a jump, dragging the affected leg behind him, and will refuse to back at all.

Treatment: The patella, if locked, can be put back into place by placing a lead line around the pastern and pulling the foot forward. As the leg is advanced the patella will bulge. If, at this point, pressure is applied to its top and back, it will click back into place. The horse will then probably move again as if nothing whatever were wrong.

The horse should be moderately exercised, to build muscle tone, but sharp turns should be avoided.

In a simple surgical procedure called a desmotomy, the veterinarian can cut the medial patellar ligament; this will prevent the patella from locking again.

Windpuffs

Definitions and Causes: Also known as windgalls, these common lesions can occur around the fetlocks of all four feet. They are formed by excessive secretion of synovial fluid. They result from strain, often of young horses in heavy training, and can affect the joint capsule, sesamoidean sheath, tarsal sheath, or flexor tendon sheath.

Windpuffs are technically classed as a mild form of synovitis (see tendosynovitis) which may be either tendinous (involving the tendons) or articular. In the latter case the capsular ligament itself is distended. Once windpuffs appear, they are generally permanent.

Symptoms: Windpuffs themselves do not cause lameness, except in the acute stage. They are fluctuant swellings which can easily be pushed aside; they tend to be firm when the horse's weight is on the leg and soft when the leg is flexed.

Windpuffs of the flexor tendon appear just above the sesamoid bones between the suspensory ligament and the flexor tendon, while articular windpuffs occur between the cannon bone and the suspensory ligament. Old cases of windpuff may become fibrosed and quite hard.

Treatment: Usually none is required after the acute stage has passed (which is a good thing since none is very effective anyhow). During the acute stage, rest, cold water and bandaging are the best therapy.

It is important to remember that although windpuffs themselves are not serious, they amy accompany a developing arthritis, bursitis, or tendonitis. In any case they are an indication that your horse's exercise regimen may have to be reexamined.

DIAGNOSIS CHART A

Symptoms	Associated Condition
STANDING	
Pointing	Foot lameness (navicular, spavin, fracture)
Blocky hoof	Advanced navicular
Heels rest lightly	Acute flexor strain
Knee bent, fetlock slightly flexed	Radial paralysis
Lowered elbow	Radial paralysis
Elbow joint semi-extended	Elbow lameness
Fetlock flexed with heel slightly raised	Sesamoiditis
IN MOTION	
Head nodding during walk	Rises when the lame front foot is on the ground
Sinking quarter in the trot	Quarter sinks on the sound side for rear leg lameness
Goes short	Pedal ostitis, navicular, shoulder lameness, bone spavin, knee lameness, sweeny
Feet put down in one piece	Navicular (late)
Goes on heels	Keratoma, ringbone (in front), coronitis, laminitis, sidebone, arthritis, seedy toe, toe crack, dropped sole
Diminshed flexion and extension of the pastern	Navicular
Swinging step	Shoulder lameness
Stiff knee	Carpitis, knee splint, acute thoroughpin
Knee not fully extended	Acute flexor strain
Hitching movement in hind limb at trot	Stifle injury
Lifts foot only slightly clear of ground	Shoulder lameness
Worsens uphill	Shoulder lameness
Worsens on soft ground	Shoulder lameness, sprain
Worsens when leg is carried	Shoulder lameness
Increases with work	Corns, splints, sesamoiditis, occult spavin, pedal ostitis, bucked shins, curb, azoturia, worms, later ringbone

LAMENESS

Symptoms	Associated Condition
Decreases with work	Bone spavin, navicular, early ringbone, stringhalt, arthritis, bursitis, pedal ostitis (decreases with light work but returns with continued work)
Difficulty in turning	Hock lameness
Sudden acute phases	Collateral ligament trouble
Intermittent	Navicular, pedal ostitis, curb, splint, bone spavin

PALPATION

Symptoms	Associated Condition
Swelling over tendons which does not pit	Sprain
Pressure deep in heel gives pain	Navicular
Coronet tender	Quittor
Hollow sound on tapping	Seedy toe
Tapping gives pain	Fracture, pedal ostitis
Rotate fetlock for pain	Fracture
Flex fetlock for pain	Osselets
Foul smell in hoof	Thrush
Heat above coronet	Foot lameness
Black spot on the white line	Abscess, gravel
Pain over the entire sole	Laminitis, fracture, large infection
Pain under frog	Navicular
Heat at coronary band	Low ringbone
Heavy pulse	Laminitis or other congestion
Heat and swelling at the pastern	Ringbone
Pastern swollen at the front	Chip fracture, osselets
Swelling over cannon bone	Bucked shins
Pain behind cannon bone	
in lower third	Suspensory ligament damage
in middle third	Inferior check ligament damage
Pain just above fetlock	Deep flexor tendon damage
Swollen knee	
in back, towards inside	Fracture of the accessory carpal bones
in front	Joint capsules
very hard	Carpitis
Point of shoulder swollen	Bicipital bursitis
Swollen hock	
towards the rear	Curb
higher	Bog spavin, thoroughpin
Swollen stifle	Gonitis

LAMENESS

DIAGNOSIS CHART B

Affected Area	Associated Problems
Foot	Laminitis, thrush, canker, puncture wounds, bruising, corns, sandcracks, keratoma, separation, pedal ostitis, contracted heels, navicular, quittor, gravel, sidebone, fracture.
Pastern	Dermatitis, ringbone, sidebone, contracted tendon, arthritis, fracture.
Fetlock	Sesamoiditis, ridge lesion, osselets, constriction of the palmar annual ligament, windpuffs, fracture.
Cannon	Sprains, splints, bowed tendons, epiphysitis, contracted tendons, bucked shins, curb (in hindleg).
Knee	Carpitis, fracture, arthritis, hygroma.
Elbow	Capped elbow, arthritis, fracture, radial paralysis.
Shoulder	Sweeny, bicipital bursitis.
Hock	Curb, bog spavin, bone spavin, thoroughpin, capped hock.
Stifle	Upward fixation of the patella, gonitis.
General	Fracture, stringhalt, azoturia, arthritis, tying up.

Bibliography

Adams, O. R., *Lameness in Horses*. Lea and Febiger, Philadelphia, 1974.

Bone, J. F. et al., *Equine Medicine and Surgery*. American Veterinary Publications, Inc., 1963.

Butler, Doug, *The Principles of Horseshoeing*. Alpine, Texas, 1974.

Hayes, M. Horace, *Veterinary Notes for Horse Owners*. Arco Publishing, Inc., New York, 1963.

Heinze, David R., "An Analysis of Navicular Disease," *American Farriers Journal*, Vol. III, issue 3, June, 1977.

Howell, A. Brazieir, *Speed in Animals: Their Specialization for Running and Leaping*. Hafner Publishing Co., New York, 1965.

Lambert, Frank Jr., "The Role of Moisture in the Physiology of the Hoof of the Harness Horse," *Veterinary Medicine/Small Animal Clinician*, April, 1966.

Lungwitz, A. and John W. Adams, *Horseshoeing*. Oregon State University Press, Corvallis, Oregon, 1966.

Milne, F. J., "Clinical Examination and Diagnosis of the diseased Equine Foot," *J.A.V.M.A.*, Vol. 151, No. 12.

Moyer, William, "Improper Shoeing" as presented at the National Horseman's Seminar, April, 1976. *Morgan Horse*, July, 1976.

Rooney, James R., *The Lame Horse*. A. S. Barnes and Co., South Brunswick and New York, 1974.

Sisson, Septimus and James Daniel Grossman, *The Anatomy of the Domestic Animals*, 4th ed. W. B. Saunders Co., Philadelphia, 1953.

Stump, John E., "Anatomy of the Normal Equine Foot, Including Microscopic Features of the Laminar Region," *J.A.V.M.A.*, Vol. 151, No. 12.

Wiseman, Robert F., *The Complete Horseshoeing Guide*. University of Oklahoma Press, Norman, Okla., 1974.

Index

Arthritis, 90-91
Azoturia, 92

Base-narrow conformation, 66, 76
Base-wide conformation, 67
Bicipital bursitis, 92
Blacksmith, 15-16
Blood vessels, 33-34
Bog spavin, 93
Bone spavin, 129-130
Bowed tendon, 93-95
Bowlegged conformation, 76
Bruising, 95-96
Bucked shins, 96
Bursitis, 96-97
　bicipital, 92
Buttress foot, 62-63

Calf knees, 72
Camped behind, 78
Camped in front, 74
Canker, 97
Canter, 58
Capped elbow, 97-98
Capped hock, 98
Club foot, 63
Conformation, 59
Constriction of the volar or plantar annular ligament, 98-99
Contracted heels, 63, 99-100
Contracted tendons, 100-101
Corns, 101-102
Cow-hocked, 76
Curb, 102-103
Cut-out under the knees, 72

Dermatitis of the pastern area, 103

Diagnosis charts, 139-141
Dropped elbow, 119-120
Dropped sole, 62

Elbow lameness, 103-104
Epiphysitis, 104

False quarter, 62
Farriers, 15-20
Fault combinations, 68-72, 76-78
Fever rings, 62
Flared foot, 61-62
Flat foot, 62
Foot, 43
Foot flight, 64
Forelegs
　bones of, 28-31
　conformation of, 65-74
　lameness of, 84-89
Forelimb, 40-41
Founder, 109-112
Fox-trot, 57
Fractures, 105-106

Gaits, 51-58
Gallop, 57-58
Gonitis, 106
Gravel, 106-107

Hindlegs
　bones of, 31-33
　conformation of, 74-80
　lameness of, 89
Hindlimb, 41-42
Hoof
　care of, 20, 47-48
　conformation of, 59-64
　description of, 43-46
Horn tumor, 108

143

INDEX

Horseshoeing, 17-18
Horseshoes, 20-25

Joint mice, 107
Joints, 35-36

Keratoma, 108
Knee lameness, 108-109
Knee-sprung, 72

Lameness, 81-83
  causes of, 82
  examination for, 84-89
  types of, 90-138
Laminitis, 109-112
Ligaments, 38
Little bones, 115-116
Locomotion, 49-51

Monday morning disease, 92
Muscles, 38

Navicular disease, 113-115
Nerves, 34

Occult spavin, 130
Open knees, 72
Osselets, 115-116

Pace, 55
Pedal osteitis, 116-117
Post-legged, 76-78
Puncture wounds, 117-118

Quittor, 119

Rack, 57
Radial paralysis, 119-120
Responsibilities of
  horseowner, 13-14
Ridge lesion, 120

Ringbone, 120-122
Rings in the hoof, 62
Running walk, 55-56

Sandcracks, 122-125
Seedy toe, 126
Separation, 126
Sesamoiditis, 126-127
Shoe boil, 97-98
Shoulder lameness, 127-128
Sickle-hocked, 76
Sidebone, 128-129
Skeleton of horse, 26-33
Spavin, 129-130
Splints, 131-132
Sprain, 132-133
Standing under in front, 74
Stay apparatus, 39-40
Stepping-pace, 57
Stifle disease, 106
Straight behind, 76
Strain, 132-133
Stringhalt, 134
Sweeny, 134

Tendons, 36-37
Thoroughpin, 135
Thrush, 135-136
Tied-in knees, 72
Toed-in conformation, 67
Trot, 54-55
Tying up syndrome, 136-137

Upward fixation of the
  patella, 137

Veterinarians, 14-15

Walk, 55
Windpuffs, 138